YOUR FAITH / YOUR COMMITMENT / GOD'S CALL

D1606613

confirm™

DIRECTOR GUIDE

APPROVED UNITED METHODIST CONFIRMATION

Confirm Director Guide

Your Faith. Your Commitment. God's Call.

Copyright © by 2016 Cokesbury

CONFIRM is an official resource for The United Methodist Church,
approved by Discipleship Ministries (General Board of Discipleship) and
published by Youth Ministry Partners and Cokesbury, The United Methodist
Publishing House, 2222 Rosa L. Parks Blvd., PO Box 280988, Nashville, TN
37228-0988.

To order copies of this publication, call toll-free 800-672-1789. You may
fax your order to 800-445-8189. Telecommunication Device for the Deaf-
Telex Telephone: 800-227-4091. Or order online at *cokesbury.com*. Use your
Cokesbury account, American Express, Visa, Discover, or MasterCard.

Writer: Rev. Tonya N. Lawrence

16 17 18 19 20 21 22 23 24 25 — 10 9 8 7 6 5 4 3 2 1

MANUFACTURED IN THE UNITED STATES OF AMERICA

Contents

Meet the Confirm Team

DEVELOPMENT EDITOR

Michael Novelli creates learner-centered resources and experiences for youth, children, and adults that explore the intersection of spiritual formation and experiential learning. Michael works as a content designer, church youth leader, and community advocate. He has an M.Ed. in Integrated Learning and is an adjunct instructor at North Park University in Chicago. Michael and his family live in Elgin, Illinois.

WRITER OF DIRECTOR GUIDE

Rev. Tonya N. Lawrence is an ordained elder in The United Methodist Church and has served several United Methodist churches in Georgia. She currently is the Associate Director for Vocational Discernment for the North Georgia Annual Conference, serves on the Board of Directors for the North Georgia Camping and Retreat Ministries, is the Co-Chair for the North Georgia Bridge to East Africa, and the Chairperson for Youth Ministry for the North Georgia Annual Conference. In addition, Rev. Lawrence is an adjunct professor at Columbia Theological Seminary in Decatur, GA. She received dual Masters degrees in Divinity and Youth Ministry from Princeton Theological Seminary in Princeton, New Jersey. Rev. Lawrence is currently working towards a Doctorate in Educational Ministry at Columbia Theological Seminary in Decatur, Georgia.

WRITER OF PARENT GUIDE

Rev. Wendy Mohler-Seib is the Director of Faith Formation for Youth and Young Adults for the Institute for Discipleship. Wendy is an ordained elder in the Great Plains Annual Conference. She is a 2001 graduate of Southwestern College with a B.A. in Religion and Philosophy and a 2012 graduate of Princeton Theological Seminary with a M.Div. and a M.A. in Youth Ministry. Wendy has served in youth ministry in churches in Kansas, Florida, and New Jersey. Wendy has also served as an associate pastor and senior pastor in Wichita, Kansas. Wendy loves preaching, teaching, and engaging in theological discussions.

WRITER OF MENTOR GUIDE

Teri Chalker holds a social work degree from the University of Kansas and a Masters in social work from Southern Illinois University at Carbondale. She worked in the medical field until she began serving on staff at Church of the Resurrection's Leawood Campus in 2003. Beginning as the elementary program director, Teri transitioned to her current role as the director of WILD1's (a fifth grade youth group) and Confirmation. Teri has been the director of Confirmation for the past nine years. She also serves as a coach for the Youth Ministry Institute.

WRITERS OF TEACHING PLANS

Kevin Alton is a full-time youth ministry creative, particularly interested in the spiritual development of youth. Among other projects, he's the co-creator of Youthworker Circuit and is excited to be part of the grant team for Science for Youth Ministry. You can find him digitally as *@thekevinalton*. Kevin lives with his family near Chattanooga, Tennessee.

Alisha Gordon, M.Div. is the Executive for Spiritual Growth, United Methodist Women. She is a sought-after writer, teacher, scholar activist, and public theologian with an interest in sharing the stories of the marginalized as a prophetic voice in the world. A native of Decatur, Georgia, Alisha holds a Bachelor of English from Spelman College and a Masters of Divinity from the Candler School of Theology at Emory University. Her unique blend of social commentary, religious engagement, and popular culture creates opportunities to use her faith and her social interests to engage in deeply meaningful conversations about race, difference, and social justice.

Ben Howard is an editor at Youth Ministry Partners. Ben graduated from Oklahoma Christian University with a degree in history and holds a Masters in Theological Studies from Lipscomb University. Prior to his work as an editor at Youth Ministry Partners, he served as a Christian Education Consultant with Cokesbury. He currently lives in Nashville, Tennessee.

Nicholas VanHorn has been a youth minister for nearly fifteen years in both the United Methodist and Episcopal traditions. He graduated from Pfeiffer University with degrees in Youth Ministry and Christian Education and from Duke Divinity with a Masters in Divinity. Nick currently resides in Winston Salem, North Carolina, with his family, where he is the Director of Youth Ministries at St. Paul's Episcopal church.

Audrey Wilder, is Director of Christian Education and Young People's Ministries for Susquehanna Conference UMC. Audrey is a graduate of High Point University with a degree in Religion and Duke Divinity School (M.Div with a certificate in Christian Education). Prior to her appointment as Director of Christian Education and Young People's Ministries, she served as the Director of Youth Ministries at First UMC, in Hershey, Pennsylvania.

CONFIRM ADVISORY TEAM
Dara Bell, Retired Conference Youth Coordinator, New Mexico Conference, UMC

Helene Foust, Associate Director of Student Ministry, Indiana Conference, UMC

Brian Hull, Assistant Professor of Youth Ministries, Asbury University

David Johnson, Associate Director, Texas Southern University, Wesley Foundation

Cindy Klick, Youth Program Director, St. Andrew UMC, Highlands Ranch, CO

Dj del Rosario, Lead Pastor, Bothell UMC, Bothell, Washington

Kate Unruh, Ph.D. student and UMC researcher, Princeton Confirmation Project

REVIEWERS

Rev. Justin Coleman, Chief Ministry Officer, The United Methodist Publishing House

Jack Radcliffe, D.Min, Lead Editor, Youth Ministry Partners

Rev. Lisa Beth White, Ph.D. Candidate, Boston University School of Theology

EDITORIAL, DESIGN, AND PRODUCTION TEAM

Jack Radcliffe, Lead Editor

Ben Howard, Associate Editor/Project Manager

Sheila K. Nimmo, Production Editing Supervisor

Pam Shepherd, Production Editor

Keely Moore, Design Manager

ADMINISTRATIVE STAFF

Brian Milford, President and CEO, The United Methodist Publishing House

Marj Pon, Associate Publisher for Teaching and Learning, The United Methodist Publishing House

Introduction

I once received a request to meet with a youth who was preparing for her senior year of high school. Because I had not seen her in a while, I suspected that there might be something important she wanted to share, but I did not know what it might be. After we talked about her grades, accomplishments in her extracurricular activities, top choices for college, and her various relationships—good and bad, our conversation meandered into her faith. To be more exact, she opened up about her struggles with her faith. She shared that she had just overcome a period during which she questioned her beliefs. I was shocked even though I did not let her know it. After all, I knew her parents, her older siblings, and many of her friends. She attended a church known for its commitment to discipleship, and she matriculated at a well-respected private school rooted in Christian values. In fact, the environment in which she lived out her life seemed ideal for nurturing a healthy faith. However, neither the perception of what was ideal nor an understanding of where things went wrong were what mattered most to me at that time. So, I continued to focus on her.

Without hesitation she got right to the point. She said, "Pastor Tonya, you know me. I always knew the answers." I was in agreement, so I enthusiastically nodded to affirm her response and continued to listen. She explained that she knew all of the answers when she was in middle school because she memorized them, which seemed fine for her life at that time. She felt secure in her level of knowing what she believed because life was simple at that age. However, when she entered high school and needed to lean on her faith, the rote answers were not enough to tether her to her beliefs so she strayed. For more than a year she made bad decisions and maintained unhealthy friendships. Then, one night a friend's life was changed by a horrific accident. She explained that it was the events of that evening that caused her to embrace her faith again, because that tragedy helped her to see how uncertain life can be. She understood that knowing about God mattered, but she realized it was more important that she feel God's presence.

I processed her words for weeks after our time together. What she was articulating in a very practical way was that a religious experience should be one that engages both head and heart and should be rooted in right answers that yield right thoughts and actions.

Inevitably in a youth-group setting someone will respond with "Jesus" as the answer to the question—any question—and it normally gets a few laughs. Without a doubt, knowing that Jesus is the answer to any of our questions about life is important. However, understanding *why* Jesus is the answer is as important if not more important.

> *Knowing that Jesus is the answer is right, but feeling that Jesus is the answer is ideal because it means Jesus has become tangible—real and personal—to the individual.*

At the Methodist Conference in 1744, John Wesley asked, "What do we teach? How do we teach it? And what do we do?" He sought to inspire individuals to a higher level of ministry and mission in the world by encouraging them to progress from contemplation about faith to believing and then ultimately to living out their faith in the world.

In line with our Wesleyan tradition, confirmation should be understood both as a "what" and "why" experience. It should be structured as a religious experience that teaches historical, theological, and doctrinal understanding of The United Methodist Church, while simultaneously being an experience that creates a space where individuals can encounter Christ through imagination, exploration, and expression.

This book offers an understanding of what confirmation is and explains why it matters. It also focuses on how to create an experience for young people that teaches the "what" and nurtures the "why" for those who are preparing to confirm their faith in Christ and their willingness to live out that faith as active members of The United Methodist Church.

"What do we teach? How do we teach it? And what do we do?" —John Wesley

What Is Confirmation?

"No one is born a Christian. One becomes a Christian through becoming a part of a community with a distinctive way of life involving definite ethical and creedal commitments."[1]

History

While the aforementioned statement is true that individuals are not born Christian but become Christian, the reality of this truth is more reflective of a time when large numbers of people were initiated into the church. At that time people were as eager to join the church as the church was eager to receive them. Once welcomed into community in the early church, individuals continued to be nurtured through religious education that was valued and taken seriously by all because of the intentionality placed upon it. As a result the church grew and was established as an integral part of the community.

Today, however, membership is declining in our churches; congregations are losing members at a greater rate than they are welcoming newcomers. Further, the understanding of the importance of religious education has waned among church leaders and members, along with the enthusiasm with which it is engaged.[2] There are many interests competing for the limited time and attention of individuals, especially youth. As a result, the church ranks low on the list of priorities for many young people today, because it has not been as enthusiastic about initiating and sustaining the interest of young people.

Yet, the words Jesus spoke in the Great Commission still stand as the gospel. According to Matthew, Jesus spoke very clearly as he stood on that mountain among those who worshiped and those who doubted. He commissioned the disciples to make disciples of others by baptizing and teaching so that the world might be transformed. Likewise, as followers, we are charged today with the task of initiating others into Christian community so that doubters will come to believe in God's presence, promises, and power and so that the entire community might be strengthened.

> *Now the eleven disciples went to Galilee, to the mountain where Jesus told them to go. When they saw him, they worshipped him, but some doubted. Jesus came near and spoke to them, "I've received all authority in heaven and on earth. Therefore, go and make disciples of all nations, baptizing them in the name of the Father and of the Son and of the Holy Spirit, teaching them to obey everything that I've commanded you. Look, I myself will be with you every day until the end of this present age." —Matthew 28:16-20.*

This section explores what Christian initiation and confirmation have meant throughout the history of the church so that we might be inspired to envision what confirmation could and should become in the future.

At one time Christian initiation was a series of seamless events that adults were eager to partake of so that they could become a part of the church. There was a time when baptism, confirmation, and the first Communion were all a part of the same ritual. Becoming a member of the church was a big deal and celebrated as such because it signified two important decisions—a personal profession of faith and a commitment to live for God. In fact, people committed to extensive and rigorous teaching both before and after they were baptized in order to remain connected to God and the church. It is important to note that this was very much an individual choice and not an obligation—well, at least initially.

Over time the commitment to and the relationship between these acts, who receives them, when they are received, and how and to what extent they are offered changed drastically. Since Jesus spoke those words, our understanding, or lack thereof, of Christian initiation—including baptism and confirmation—and how these practices have been influenced by the political climate, cultural shifts, and technological advancements has taken on different meaning (as discussed later in this section).

Although baptisms still occur, the subsequent teaching, understanding of, and living out of that covenant has lost much of its importance. As a result, confirmation, now a separate event, has in turn lost its sacredness among those who came to believe that baptism was the only means necessary for Christian initiation.

While this can be successfully argued for adults, who are baptized and can respond for themselves, it is not the case for infants and children whose parents/guardians respond on their behalf. Salvation is still personal. Confirmation is important at the appropriate time so that these individuals, for whom someone else responded earlier, can offer a personal response to their faith in Jesus Christ and a willingness to become faithful members of The United Methodist Church through the offering of their prayers, presence, gifts, witness, and service.

Before we get too far along in our understanding of what confirmation is today, we must consider what confirmation meant to the church, people, and society at different points in the history of Christianity. As we journey through our history, you will notice that over time shifts occurred in the age at which one was baptized, the reason one was baptized, and the relationship between baptism and confirmation.

In *The Theology of Confirmation in Relation to Baptism*, Gregory Dix, an Anglican priest, said that the shifts in our understanding of Christian initiation rituals along with the "benefits" have been watered down over the years to the extent that people today associate "Baptism vaguely with vaccination and Confirmation with leaving school."[3] Christian initiation, including confirmation, was not always viewed as a dreaded experience that one just "had to get through" in the way that it is viewed today. While it's true that no one is born Christian, "becoming a part of the community"—Christian initiation—has clearly lost some of its distinction and definition over time.

As we move forward in our understanding of what confirmation should be, we must solidify our view of confirmation and its potential for discipleship-making so that we can help parents and students move from dread to excitement. Let us now explore Christian initiation, including confirmation during the early church, the Middle Ages, the Reformation, the early days in America, the Industrial Revolution, and today.

The Early Church (Through the Fifth Century)

In the early church, Christian initiation meant committing to be a part of an experiential way of life that was radically different from the dominant culture. Initiation into this community consisted of extensive education, which sometimes lasted up to three years, and was then followed by a sequence of sacramental events including baptism, confirmation, public profession, and then, the Eucharist.[4] To be more specific, baptism was followed by an anointing, a sealing with the sign of the cross and the laying on of hands which confirmed the believers *metanoia*, or "change of heart," and involvement in ministry as symbolized by the broken bread and spilled wine at the Communion table.[5]

After the all-encompassing sacramental system of initiation was conferred upon individuals, they were full-fledged members in the church of Jesus Christ. These new converts were to be spirit-filled and powerfully different from those persons who continued to live their lives based on the dominant culture.[6] They were expected to carry forward the mission of disciple-making.

Even though there was initial excitement among those new members, leaders in the early church realized that after the membership was attained through this climactic experience, enthusiasm quickly waned because the dominant culture was too strong to resist. Hearts that turned in towards the church turned outwards again, reverting to their previous way of life.

To counter this, leaders created intentional structures to nurture and encourage new converts in their faith.[7] So, education continued in order for people to grow in their faith and their relationship with God. According to Walter Brueggemann, our Jewish ancestors viewed education as a means of encountering God as well as a means of passing along traditions among young people.[8] The church created a means by which individuals could be strengthened through an acquaintance with God. Confirmation, a part of this process of Christian initiation, was offered with the hope that individuals would have an encounter with God. This encounter should still be the emphasis today.

Things were going well in the expansion of Christianity until the fourth century, when Constantine mandated Christianity as a state-approved religion. This decision drastically changed the way that confirmation was understood, which ultimately changed how it was offered. Rather than being confirmed into the church because one had experienced a change of heart and wanted to live differently, individuals joined the church so that they could earn a living. Yes, under Constantine's rule, church membership was politicized.

During Constantine's reign, membership in the church came with social privileges. Becoming Christian was now a requirement for employment. As you can imagine, church membership increased significantly because of this. It did not take long before there was a "waiting list" for initiation. Unfortunately, however, those who were initiated only for political reasons reverted to business as usual once they received employment. Churches, "swollen" by the influx, were left with inflated rolls consisting of individuals who were members in name only. Those who did not take their faith seriously became "bored" with their understanding of Christian initiation and they checked out. This tarnished the image of the church.[9] Those who joined for the wrong reasons quickly left, creating doubt among onlookers and calling into question the validity of the entire experience and its significance.

The Middle Ages (Fifth Century— Fifteenth Century)

Another significant shift that occurred in the early times of the church was the separation of the events in the initiation process. By the end of the sixth century, concern had grown over children's souls of the state-approved Christians because they had not yet been baptized. So infant baptism was established. Saint Augustine's theology and the fear of infants dying before they were baptized caused a major shift in how initiation occurred. Infants were baptized within the first few days of their birth.[10] It was believed that God's grace was available to all, even those who could not respond for themselves. As Methodists, we refer to this as prevenient grace—that which is available before we become aware of or acknowledge it. During this time they also began to offer Communion for infants who were baptized. The pastor would place the Communion elements on his finger which would then be placed in the infant's mouth.

While it seemed great to include the youngest among them to be baptized, this caused challenges for the sacramental system that had been previously established. Infants could be baptized and receive Communion with the help of others, but they could not be confirmed because confirmation is an individual act. As a result, confirmation was separated from what was once a seamless system of events and delayed

18   Confirm Director Guide

until young people could respond for themselves, causing the connection within the sacramental system to be broken, literally and figuratively. What was once joined with baptism and Holy Communion was removed. From that time forward, confirmation would never again be viewed at the same level of importance.

Confirmation became a "member intake" process for children of adult believers so that they too could receive the bounty of the state and the promise of the church. It was separated from baptism and offered to children at age seven.[11] As all of these changes were occurring, the meaning of membership was still shifting. Also the notion of education as a means of continued nurture and encouragement was evolving.

Reformation (Sixteenth Century)

Confirmation was even further defined during the Protestant Reformation. Reformers such as Martin Luther viewed baptism and Holy Communion to be the only two sacraments because those were the only acts that could be traced back to Jesus. "The Protestant churches, which developed out of the Reformation in the sixteenth century, rejected the idea of confirmation as a sacrament."[12]

Many theological leaders at this time contributed to the redefinition of this act. Soren Kierkegaard considered it "a triviality" because it had been watered down to serve merely as a gateway into adulthood where young people received the right to vote, "work, join a guild, attend a state school, or go off to boarding school." Confirmation became a set of classes, a celebration of the "great festival of youth," an examination, a confession of faith, and the memorization of a biblical passage.[13] Because there were so many different understandings of confirmation at the time, random customs became associated with it. For example, during the service of confirmation, students were encouraged to leave the chancel rail to seek out their parents in the congregation in order to ask for their forgiveness and blessing.[14] Acts like this were not originally a part of initiation but became a part of the watered-down version. The focus was no longer fully on God; emphasis was now placed on an individual.

John Calvin considered it "misborn wraith" and Martin Luther considered it nothing more than "monkey business." [15] John Wesley, our founder, also had definite thoughts of confirmation that were not too far removed from these church leaders (as seen in a later discussion).

As a result of this new way of thinking about Christianity that was separate and apart from the Catholic Church, the Calvinist, Lutheran, and Anglican traditions emphasized the necessity of catechesis—the teaching of faith to those who have been baptized as infants over confirmation. [16] Confirmation, then, became a ceremony for those who had learned the catechism and other basics of faith publicly professed in Christian commitment. Because we stem from Anglican roots, it is important to note that "when John Wesley revised the *Anglican Book of Common Prayer* to serve as a worship book for North American Methodists, he omitted confirmation completely." [17]

Methodists in America Without Clergy (1784)

The meaningfulness of confirmation did not fare well among Methodists who were settling in America. With the new settlers, Methodism entered a world that was much different from its roots in Great Britain. Initially, there was a clear connection to British Methodists. However, after the Revolutionary War ended in 1783, American Methodists were no longer able to receive Communion from the Anglican churches because the ties with the British had been cut.

Because of this change, no ordained ministers were available to offer the sacraments for a more than one year. During this time, worship consisted primarily of preaching, singing, Bible reading, and praying, which weakened the balance they had originally hoped to maintain. John Wesley, founder of the Methodist movement, knew this had to be resolved because of his belief in the connection of the means of grace and personal piety. So, in December of 1784, the Christmas Conference was convened in Baltimore to ordain American Methodist ministers who would be able to administer the sacraments. But the "damage" had already been done. Disconnected from England, Methodists were now focused less on the sacraments and more on the individual experience of salvation.[18]

Therefore, confirmation, now only a loose extension of baptism, became even more ambiguous when the sacramental meaning and significance of baptism was lost. According to Gayle Felton, there was a time when Methodists held together "sacramentalism," which attracted people to the faith.[19] However, when Methodism came to America, the emphasis on the sacraments changed and minimized the importance of confirmation even more. Because of Wesley's intentional omission of the confirmation service from the *Anglican Book of Common Prayer* and the absence of Methodist clergy to administer the rituals, neither the sacraments nor confirmation were practiced.

Twentieth Century (Industrial Revolution)

While it is true that Luther objected to the flawed system, he did believe that it provided people with a path of discipleship. This system "provided pastoral care in a comprehensive way to deeply felt human needs"[20] that are permanent. Likewise, in The United Methodist Church today, we acknowledge the sacraments of baptism and Holy Communion, but the need for pastoral care still exists. Members in churches need a path of discipleship that meets their needs along all ages and stages of life's journey. By the 1950s and 1960s, confirmation language began to reappear. By 1964, a service of confirmation was added to *The United Methodist Hymnal* as a part of the baptismal service.

Today

Confirmation, also casually referred to as "joining the church," is viewed today as a "last chance of the church" to save the faith of young people and cement them to a pew for life. Yet it has the potential to be so much more. [21] In large part this is because confirmation remains misunderstood.

In my experience, parents view confirmation as the "saving grace" for their children before the magnetic pull of society gets a hold of them and draws them away from the church. Simultaneously, most young people view confirmation as something they would never do without the coaxing of their parents. While the pressure that parents place on teens regarding confirmation is incorrect, they are correct in viewing it as a grace-filled experience.

Historically, confirmation was a big deal in the Christian community because it welcomed, educated, nurtured, and discipled as an extension of both the baptismal covenant and the Great Commission. Today, confirmation allows us the opportunity to help congregations understand their role in welcoming, educating, and discipling young people. Furthermore, confirmation offers us the opportunity to help parents understand their role in welcoming, educating, nurturing, and discipling their adolescents.

There has been a lot of change in confirmation over the years. In fact, there has been so much change in how we understand confirmation that individuals—parents and students—are not quite sure what it means or why it matters today. This highly regarded act that was once a part of the sacramental system of initiation that included baptism and Holy Communion has become a disconnected afterthought— if thought of at all. While this lack of understanding is more than likely the reason many youth are reluctant to participate, it should be our impetus for making the connection between the two acts.

Although we do not ascribe to the same theology as that of the Roman Catholic Church that still regards baptism, confirmation, and Holy Communion as sacraments, as United Methodists we should understand that each of these steps plays an important role in the discipleship process. Rooted in the beliefs of our founder John Wesley, we believe that there are only two sacraments—baptism and Holy Communion—because they were the only two ordained by Christ our Lord in the gospel.[22] Even though we do not consider confirmation to be sacramental, we should understand and convey its importance. Throughout one's Christian life—from baptism to burial—education should be offered to encourage active and enthusiastic engagement in the journey of discipleship. Confirmation should be understood as an important part of the journey for young people who need to claim Christ for themselves.

It is our hope that an understanding of the history of confirmation will encourage you to evaluate how confirmation is currently being offered in your context so that you can envision how much more confirmation could be for the young people in your church. The view of confirmation can be revitalized with understanding of its purpose and some enthusiasm and intentionality placed upon its facilitation. Now, let's turn our attention to why discipleship is necessary.

History of Adolescence

"Our society has passed from a period which was ignorant of adolescence to a period in which adolescence is the favorite age. We now want to come to it early and linger in it as long as possible." —Philippe Ariés [23]

While in seminary, I read a book that changed my way of thinking about adolescence: *The Case Against Adolescence*. The book was required reading by Kenda C. Dean, one of my professors. I was initially turned off by the title of this book, even though I knew the course was taught by one of

23

the world's strongest advocates for young people. I also was aware that the primary objective of the course was to explore various approaches to youth ministry. Since I also was an advocate for young people, I did not understand how this book related to my passion for them. However, before delving into methods, we had to read this book. Although reluctantly, I did so. I was pleasantly surprised by what I discovered. In the first few pages, I realized the book was not arguing against the importance of young people. It was, in fact, arguing *for* the importance, ingenuity, inclusion, and involvement of young people. It was speaking my language and I loved it.

Perhaps you are wondering what the history of adolescence has to do with confirmation—just as I wondered about the content of the book I had to read. If so, I understand. However, it is my hope that you will keep reading and also discover something meaningful.

> *"Confirmation is a sacrament that communicates the fullness of the Holy Spirit, strengthens confirmands and allows them to take up the tasks of Christian life with greater maturity."*
> *— Thomas Aquinas* [24]

As we know, confirmation is not a sacrament for United Methodists, but it can be used as a vehicle to strengthen the faith of confirmands and encourage them in their Christian life. Understanding how to strengthen young people in their faith is one of the major dilemmas faced by the church today. In an age when young people are disinterested in the church, and the responsibility of parents to care for young people has been extended well into the young adult age range, the development and strengthening of our young people is needed now more than ever. It is also more challenging than ever.

However, this was not always the case. It never occurred to me that adolescence (as we know it today) has not always existed. Indeed, we have all lived through the angst-filled prepubescent and pubescent years, but the way we progress through those years today is not the same as it used to be. The term *adolescence* was created as a result of modern industrialization.[25]

Prior to the Industrial Era (1880–1920s), young people worked alongside adults as soon as they were able.[26] Doing so provided young people with opportunities for both life and vocational skill development. This work also provided young people with a sense of belonging in community and a sense of self-worth as a contributor to that same community. Throughout most of human history, young people were integrated into adult society early.

Without the same opportunities for skill development, young people were left to find ways to occupy their interests and curiosities. Over time, wayward behavior developed among this age group. And, as a result, laws were created to regulate young people who were once included in society.[27] Not only was their labor restricted by these new laws but also their development. Companies identified these young people with nothing to do as a new niche and began to mass produce toys and games to occupy their time. Also, playing with dolls became popular for young men in this age group when Hasbro created toys like the G.I. Joe doll.[28]

As a result of the changes in labor laws, these young people who were once independent but involved in the community had been stripped of their independence and disengaged from the community. These young people who were once considered "small adults" were now infantilized and considered "larger children."[29] This was a period of regression for the younger people in society — a society that was in need of more than mere games and dolls for entertainment. During this time period, childhood was extended, which also meant that adulthood was delayed.[30]

While this chapter helps to frame our understanding of the shift in young people from independent individuals who contributed to the community to dependent young people who were viewed as a distraction by the community, we must be mindful that this historical perspective represents a specific population. This perspective reflects the "coming of age" experience for European Americans, the majority population, but does not fully represent the "coming of age" experience of African American, Asian American, Latino/a, and Native American young people.

As we consider the intentionality with which other ethnicities reared young people to understand their particular culture as well as the broader culture, we must also consider how this history can inform us today. With the shifts in the distribution of demographic populations, there is an opportunity for us to be shaped by perspectives that are different from one's own.

For the populations that were not in the majority at this time in history, spiritual, social, and psychological development was different. Not only did the young people in these populations have to establish and navigate their identity within their particular context, but also they had to establish and navigate their identity in the majority culture. This is of significance because the age at which individuals are confirmed is pivotal for developing a healthy sense of identity. According to Erik Erikson, in puberty and adolescence an individual who is experiencing a physical maturity is also seeking to understand his/her new social role.[31] He states further that an individual should be allowed to integrate various identities acquired up to that point in order to acquire a sense of belonging that is necessary for a person to develop a healthy sense of self.[32]

In each of the aforementioned communities of color, churches, schools, and parents recognized this. These entities worked together in order to help young people develop a level of consciousness that would allow them to function in and out of different contexts.[33] While each of these populations holds this non-European American factor in common, its history cannot be lumped together under one umbrella with the other communities of color.

Each is uniquely positioned from the others and has its own particularities which should be understood and honored.

The church community played a significant role in the development of its young people, particularly for African Americans who had to rely on faith in order to endure some of the most challenging experiences in United States history.[34] From slavery to segregation to Jim Crow, the church helped to offer a sense of belonging that the community did not. According to Lincoln and Mamiya, "in the interaction between these two major institutional sectors of family and church, there has always existed a historical tradition of special caring for young [people]."[35]

"Black churches have always provided a community and an atmosphere where people could be affirmed and accepted as they are." — C. Eric Lincoln and Lawrence H. Mamiya[36]

Historically, black churches have nurtured survival skills while also developing educational opportunities.[37] Because people derive knowledge from their social context, which in turn contributes to their individual and communal horizons of religious meaning,[38] the Black Church has always sought "to empower the individual to value oneself while living in a society that does not."[39] There are experiences that are unique to black persons—cultural and historical—that shape the black perspective on the African American Christian experience.[40] One of the major functions of black churches is to offer a communal *eros* that allows individuals to become fully human.[41]

Though the intentionality to develop a healthy sense of self and belonging while navigating different contexts is true in the black church for African Americans, I believe that it is also true in Asian American congregations, Latino/a congregations, and Native American congregations. Such an understanding informs the "what," "why," and "how" not only in confirmation with young people but also in all ministry with young people. Therefore, as we consider the broader historical perspective of young people, we must also consider the experiences of others because that understanding matters in creating a meaningful confirmation experience for each person.

While early reformers dismissed the act of confirmation, they maintained a firm position that a proper education on the doings of the church was necessary for every baptized believer. [42] As we consider the state of young people and their interest in the church today, we cannot be dismissive of confirmation; it is a sacred time in which an understanding and valuing of self can occur. It should be a time when young people can explore and better understand who they are in relationship to others and begin to negotiate their sense of self within that understanding.

Confirmation should empower students to develop relationships with peers and adults, encounter God in a more meaningful way, and learn about the history, polity, and doctrine of Methodism. Confirmation is also an opportunity for the church to build a solid youth ministry program, develop young leaders who will one day desire to chair major committees in the church because "doing no harm, doing good, and attending to the ordinances of God" has been instilled in their hearts.

According to Epstein, young people are capable thinkers who can love, be tough, be creative, and handle responsibility. To this list, I would add that they are imaginative, in tune with cultural trends and, as a result, are very capable of breathing new ways of ministry into the church. Needless to say, the book mentioned earlier that I originally doubted has impacted the way I think about, design, and do ministry with young people. It was proof for me that you truly cannot judge a book by its cover, a lesson I now apply to every young person I encounter because everyone has gifts to be discovered and shared. [43] Confirmation is a great time to allow such realizations to be manifested.

In a church I once served, there was a strong tradition of confirmation. The parents readily signed up their reluctant preteens. However, these preteens did not remain reluctant. From the moment they entered the confirmation experience, I viewed them as "small adults" who had a lot to offer the church rather than "older children" who needed to fall in line with things as they were.

As a result, after two years of nine-month confirmation classes, the choir that was once nonexistent made a comeback. The first Sunday of its return, there were over seventy young voices singing praises to God from the choir loft. In addition to that, students who were confirmed the first year returned to "help assist" the second year. Youth developed a passion to engage in the church, and they were encouraged to do so. Furthermore, youth were serving beyond the local church on CCYM and at other conference-level events—including as retreat leaders and annual conference delegates. The label and stifling that we have attached to this age group does not have to be the case—it *should not* be the case. Young people are quite capable. I believe that my view of them as capable individuals helped shape how they viewed themselves in the life of their church.

> • What is something you learned in this section that will make a difference in how you approach confirmation?

Confirmation and Rites of Passage in Other Traditions

As we consider confirmation in the United Methodist tradition, it is also important to consider what confirmation looks like in other traditions. Ask yourself the following questions and jot down a few thoughts on the next page.

• What can other faith traditions teach us about our personal beliefs?

• What can other cultures reveal to us about what we do, how we do it, and why we do it?

During my first semester of seminary, I read *Coming of Age in Samoa* by Margaret Mead, an American cultural anthropologist. In her book, Mead sought reasons for the difficulties that teens, specifically young women, were facing by studying a culture different from that which was prevalent in the US in the early twentieth century. Consider the following:

> *"The traveler who has been once from home is wiser than he [she] who has never left his [her] own door step, so a knowledge of one other culture should sharpen our ability to scrutinize more steadily, to appreciate more lovingly, our own."* —*Margaret Mead* [44]

As an advocate for social change, Mead did not go to Samoa simply to study Samoans; she went to gain understanding of how culture shapes individuals as a precursor to her understanding of the whole human race. [45] For Mead, the ideal culture was one that produced happy and "emotionally sturdy people; one that found a place for every human gift." [46] As a result of Mead's observations in Samoa, she was able to conclude that adolescence is not necessarily a time of stress and strain, per se, but it is the cultural conditions experienced during adolescence that make the stress and strain so. [47] As a result of her experience, Mead realized that many of the challenging psychological experiences a person faces during the adolescent developmental stage are shaped by cultural demands and expectations.

Confirm Director Guide

With both a passion and concern for the well-being of young people and the culture that impacts them, I was intrigued by the words that leapt off the pages of Mead's book and harmonized with my spirit. The seed had been planted. I became curious about how young people are reared in other cultures and also about what I could learn if I observed the culture of another for myself.

I became interested by the intersection between the gospel of Jesus Christ and culture in an African context.[48] I also became interested in the cultural traditions of Ghanaians and their valuing of and commitment to their youth through customs like rites of passage which are performed mainly for young women.[49] I was aware of a few rites of passage programs that were being conducted in the US. I was even aware of one being conducted in my home church that focused on social etiquette and manners. I, however, was seeking something more meaningful—something that could impact an individual's relationship with Christ and the understanding of himself or herself within society.

I immersed myself in Ghanaian culture in order to study not only rites of passage for young girls but also the family systems, ministry with youth, and the intersection between the church and culture. Their rearing process seemed more substantive and therefore, more intentional, than that which was being offered in the US.

According to Arnold van Gennep, rites of passage, also referred to as a liminal phase, is an initiation rite which "accompanies every change of place, state, social position, and age."[50] A complete scheme of rites of passage includes the following three phases:

- a preliminal phase of separation

- a liminal phase of transition

- a postliminal phase of incorporation.[51]

Because liminality is a time of transition, the first and third stages of this rite of passage are stable, but the middle phase represents a time of flux and limbo. Or, to say it another way, the first and third stages respectively represent the current stage of being and the future stage to which one will belong. The middle stage of transition is the becoming stage in which understanding about life questions are being answered.

Dipo, the African rite of passage that I studied, is intentionally designed to guide adolescent females through their time of flux with the help of elder Krobo women. It ensures they are provided with instruction and knowledge to aid them in successfully crossing over the threshold into womanhood.

Although Dipo is considered a pagan ritual, it has a pulse on the community and strives to challenge cultural norms and societal issues through the proper rearing of the community's young women, but their custom lacks a connection to Christ. Conversely, the Ghanaian church offers Christ in abundance as well as a confirmation experience, but has stripped its coming of age process of any gender differentiation and preparation. Dipo is a joint production incorporating the experiences of many people. It consists of an "ordered sequence of groups of activities that individually enhance ritual efficacy and collectively lead up to a heightened peak of ritual performance."[52]

Based on my experience with various confirmation classes and the Ghanaian rites of passage, I believe there is a better way of fostering a healthy identity of formation. Confirmation should be thought of as more than an academic experience within the limits of the Christian calendar. It should not be that thing that is dreaded by parents and youth alike. Instead, confirmation should be viewed as an opportunity to encounter God.

Considering the characteristics of Dipo rites of passage in Ghana in relationship to confirmation, I believe they each have some things in common. Similar to confirmation, Dipo has changed with the times. It was originally designed to last for three years in order to properly teach the young women how to manage the home, as well as care for their family and themselves. However, because of technological advancements and cultural changes, the rites have morphed.

I also believe there are some things from this process that can be considered in how we offer confirmation.

- First, these young women were never alone.

- Secondly, these young ladies were officially declared women in several ways.

- Finally, they were celebrated before, during, and after the Dipo process.

I believe that adolescents in the US could benefit from such intentionality and that our society could be transformed by such a process.

According to Arnold van Gennep, the stages of transformation are:

- separation

- margin (transition)

- reaggragation (incorporation) [53]

Missing from this three-pronged approach, however, are clearly defined entry and exit points. Without such, transition could be a stage without end, an adolescence that extends beyond one's teenage years into the twenties or thirties. Or, to say it differently, an endless phase of transition could render a young person inactive in the church or disconnected completely. Confirmation could serve as one of those clearly defined markers for a young person seeking identity today.

Even though confirmation is not an end to the journey,
it does symbolize a personal profession of faith and a
realization that one is committed to their faith development.

According to Richard Osmer, young people must complete
the following tasks over time in order to function fully as
adults in a highly differentiated, loosely bound society.

• They must renegotiate their relationship with family.

• They must acquire a repertoire of knowledge and skills
necessary to participate in the instructional contexts that
characterize modernity.

• They must construct a personal system of moral meaning
in response to the challenges posed by cultural pluralism,
generational discontinuity, and instrumental reason. [54]

Not only must they find the answer to the "Who am I?"
question, but also they must seek understanding for the
"How do I maneuver society so that I can find where I fit in?"
question. Simply put, they must develop a sense of self.

My experience in West Africa confirmed the words of
Margaret Mead. By experiencing the coming of age process
for young women in Ghana, I developed distinct views of
how much more impactful confirmation could be in the US.
Through this experience, I gained a new sense of hope for
young people, the church, and our society.

Between baptism and Holy Communion is confirmation. Just
as individuals are encouraged to remember their baptism
and to also remember the acts of Jesus Christ who died
for each of us, they should also be able to remember their
confirmation experience "fondly" and as meaningful to their
journey of formation.

Confirmation Traditions in the US Today

In Roman Catholicism, confirmation remains one of the seven sacraments. Results of confirmation include grace that:

- strengthens one's faith;

- draws a person closer to Christ;

- increases the effectiveness of spiritual gifts;

- and makes a person an effective witness for Jesus Christ.

After confirmation, individuals are also able to receive Communion. In this tradition, confirmation is viewed as a necessary step before Communion, just as it was required in the early church.

Other Protestant Traditions

Our brothers and sisters in other mainline protestant denominations (Presbyterian, Lutheran, etc.) also have a confirmation process that is similar in many ways to that of The United Methodist Church. However, our Baptist brothers and sisters do not have a confirmation process because of their theological views regarding the age at which one is baptized. In the Baptist tradition, individuals are baptized at an age when they are able to respond in the profession of faith for themselves. This is known as "believer's baptism." There is no infant baptism. Therefore, the personal profession that we celebrate as a confirmation is not necessary because it is done at baptism.

Jewish Tradition

In the Jewish tradition, "coming of age" is marked by a specific age. When a boy reaches the age of thirteen and a girl the age of twelve, he or she celebrates Bar/Bat Mitzvah.

There is, however, extensive preparation that occurs up to a year in advance of that special day and involves the Rabbi, congregation, and the parents/family. During the time of preparation, individuals learn a portion of the Torah which is recited during their ceremony.

Another key feature of this "coming of age" process is the involvement of the family prior, during, and after the event. Since a Bar or Bat Mitzvah celebration is part of a process, not an isolated event, the year leading up to the ceremony is an opportunity for the family to learn, experience, and grow together. Finally, the Jewish ceremony affirms a person's identity with a people, which is something that many young people seek today.

Mexican Tradition for Girls (Also Celebrated in Other Latin American Traditions)

Quinceanera is a tradition that celebrates young girls when they reach the age of fifteen. The term is derived from the Spanish words *quince* and *anos,* which define the meaning of the celebration as the fifteenth year. The festival origins are shrouded in the history of the Mexican people. As with so many things Mexican, it combines both Spanish-Catholic traditions.

While there are many ceremonies that mark the passages through the stages of life, Quinceanera is among the most important. It includes the mother and other women of the community as they instruct the girl in her duties and responsibilities, urging her to follow the correct path in her life, while remaining true to her people and their traditions.[55]

This coming of age traditionally begins with a Catholic mass during which the girl renews her baptismal vows and recommits to her family and her faith. Not only is there a celebration in the church but also a huge fiesta for family and friends following this event.[56]

Confirm Director Guide

While the roots of this tradition are found in Mexican culture and are related to the Catholic Church, Quinceanera is also celebrated in Puerto Rican, Cuban, and other Latino cultures and other faith traditions. There is a blessing for a Quinceanera in *The United Methodist Book of Worship* (No. 534).

Today, Hispanics (Latinos) are the largest and youngest minority group in the US.[57] While not a replacement for confirmation, a Quinceanera blessing could be a way of nurturing young girls and honoring the baptismal covenant. Asbury UMC in Flint, Michigan, did exactly that. According to the pastor, Rev. Tommy McDoniel, in this instance (see endnote 58), "the quinceanera worship and celebration was an event to treasure in the life of their church because the members of the congregation responded to their covenantal promises along with [the young girl's] parents by pulling together to make the event happen."[58]

We are charged today with the task of initiating others into Christian community so that doubters will come to believe in God's presence, promises, and power.

Chapter One Endnotes

1. James F. White, *Introduction to Christian Worship,* Third Edition (Nashville: Abingdon Press, 2001); 203.

2. Charles R. Foster, *From Generation to Generation: The Adaptive Challenge of Mainline Protestant Education in Forming Faith* (Eugene, Or.: Wipf and Stock Publishers); 9.

3. Dom Gregory Dix, *The Theology of Confirmation in Relation to Baptism* (Westminster: Dacre Press, 1946); 40. A public lecture at the University of Oxford, January 1946.

4. White, *Christian Worship*, 203.

5. William Myers, ed., *Becoming and Belonging: A Practical Design for Confirmation* (Cleveland, Ohio: United Church Press, 1993); 5.

6. Ibid., 5.

7. Vygotsky would call this scaffolding.

8. Walter Brueggemann, *The Creative Word: Canon as a Model for Biblical Education* (Philadelphia: Fortress Press, 1982); 1.

9. Myers, *Becoming*, 5.

10. White, *Christian Worship*, 212.

11. Meyers, *Becoming*, 6.

12. Gayle Carlton Felton, *By Water and the Spirit: Making Connections for Identity and Ministry* (Nashville, Tn.: Discipleship Resources, 1997); 37.

13. Myers, *Becoming*, 7.

14. Ibid., 7.

15. Richard Robert Osmer, *Confirmation: Presbyterian Practices in Ecumenical Perspective* (Louisville, Ky.: Geneva Press, 1996); 58.

16. Felton, *By Water and the Spirit*, 37.

17. Ibid.

18. Ibid., 4.

19. Ibid.

20. White, *Introduction to Christian Worship*, 189.

21. Myers, ed., *Becoming and Belonging*, 3.

22. Sacraments are "by which [God] doth work invisibly in us, and doth not only quicken, but also strengthen and confirm our faith in him." From *The Book of Discipline of The United Methodist Church, 2012.* Copyright © 2012 by The United Methodist Publishing House; ¶104, page 67. Used by permission.

23. Philippe Aries as quoted in Robert Epstein, *Case Against Adolescence: Rediscovering the Adult in Every Teen* (Sanger, CA.: Quill Driver Books/Word Dancer Press, 2007); 25.

24. Thomas Aquinas as quoted in Osmer, *Confirmation: Presbyterian Practices*, 30.

25. Epstein, *Case Against Adolescence*, 23.

26. Ibid.

27. Ibid., 24.

28. Ibid., 66.

29. Ibid., 25.

30. Ibid., 5.

31. Erik H. Erikson, *Identity and the Life Cycle* (New York: W.W. Norton & Co., Inc., 1980); 94.

32. Ibid., 95.

33. Known as *Double Consciousness* in the African American community; coined by W.E.B. Du Bois to describe those whose identity is divided into facets in order to assimilate into and out of different cultural contexts. See W.E.B. Du Bois, *The Souls of Black Folk* (New York: Dover Publications, 1903).

34. The history of the black church experience is highlighted because it has been researched and written about more extensively than that of other populations.

35. C. Eric Lincoln and Lawrence H. Mamiya, *The Black Church in the African American Experience* (Durham and London: Duke University Press, 1990); 310.

36. Ibid., 316.

37. Dale P. Andrews, *Practical Theology for Black Churches* (Louisville, Ky.: John Knox Press, 2002); 2.

38. Ibid., 33.

39. Ibid., 24.

40. Ibid., 24.

41. Peter J. Paris, *The Social Teaching of the Black Churches* (Philadelphia, PA: Fortress Press, 1985); 59.

42. Osmer, *Confirmation: Presbyterian Practices,* 31.

43. Margaret Mead, *Coming of Age in Samoa: A Psychological Study of Primitive Youth for Western Civilization* (New York: Perennial Classics, 2001); xvii.

44. Ibid., 11.

45. Ibid., xvii.

46. Ibid., xvi.

47. Ibid., 161.

48. *Gospel and Culture in an African Context* was taught in Fall 2007 at Princeton Theological Seminary, Princeton New Jersey, by Rev. Dr. Cephas Omenyo, a visiting professor from the University of Ghana, in Ghana, West Africa.

49. Ibid.

50. Arnold van Gennep as quoted in *The Ritual Process*, Victor Turner (Ithaca: Cornell University Press, 1989); 94.

51. Arnold van Gennep, *The Rites of Passage* (Chicago: The University of Chicago Press, 1960); 11.

52. Joseph K. Adjaye, *Boundaries of Self and Other in Ghanaian Popular Culture* (Westport, CT.: Praeger Publishers, 2004); 65.

53. van Gennep, *Rites of Passage*, xii.

54. Osmer, *Confirmation: Presbyterian Practices,* 11.

55. "The Quinceanera Celebration," *http://www.learnnc.org/lp/editions/chngmexico/218*. Accessed 30 July 2016.

56. *https://www.globalcitizen.org/en/content/13-amazing-coming-of-age-traditions-from-around-th/*. Accessed 30 July 2016.

57. *http://www.pewhispanic.org/2009/12/11/between-two-worlds-how-young-latinos-come-of-age-in-america/*. Accessed 30 July 2016.

58. *http://news.michiganumc.org/2010/10/flint-asbury-umc-holds-quinceanera-celebration/*. Accessed 30 July 2016.

Theology of Confirmation

"Theology must be the presupposition to any
curriculum." —Randolph Crump Miller [1]

One of the things that I enjoy most about the very first
confirmation class every year is the encounter with the young
person who clearly does not want to be there. He or she
normally sits in the back of the room with eyes fixed upon
whatever is going on outside the nearest door or window and
reluctantly provides answers that are generally short, and
perhaps even inaudible.

As off-putting as this student's actions can be, he or she is
one of my favorite "types" of student to encounter. I know
that the initial resistance, while hard fought, will wane as he
or she begins to open up over the course of the confirmation
experience. Perhaps you have encountered this type of
student also. An experience with a reluctant student reminds
us of the limitations of our role as teachers in relationship
to the limitless ability of God's mysterious work through the
Holy Spirit. This type of experience should also underscore
the importance of creating a confirmation experience in
which God can work.

The Great Commission is foundational to the understanding
of confirmation and should be infused in how the experience
is structured. Our mission is to baptize and then teach for
transformation. Although baptism is an event that happens
only once and should be remembered, teaching is ongoing.
As confirmation leaders, our role is to offer young people
the opportunity to affirm for themselves the desire to live in
Christian community, help them to understand and embrace
our rich Methodist traditions and beliefs, and encourage

them to be open to the Holy Spirit. Confirmation is an important part of a person's spiritual journey and to building vital congregations. Our task is to help others—students, parents, and the whole of the congregation—to understand that confirmation truly is sacred.

As we turn our attention to the theology of confirmation, I would like to invite you to reflect upon the following questions:

• First, what Scripture verse undergirds your beliefs about confirmation?

• Secondly, how do you understand God to be involved in the confirmation experience?

• Finally, why have you chosen to teach/lead the confirmation experience?

As much as individuals question the meaning and importance of confirmation today, we must help them to understand that it is an opportunity to encounter God. According to *The Book of Discipline*, "[t]heology is our effort to reflect upon God's gracious action in our lives," the church, and the world. These theological reflections should give "expression to the mysterious reality of God's presence, peace, and power" so that we may "articulate more clearly our understanding of the divine-human encounter" and be prepared more fully "to participate in God's work in the world."[2]

As United Methodists, we are called to identify the needs both of individuals and of society and to address those needs out of the resources of our Christian faith in a way that is clear, convincing, and effective. In order to do so we, as United Methodists of every age and stage, should have a personal understanding of God. Thus, our theological task as believers should be both critical and constructive, individual and communal, contextual and incarnational, and essentially practical. Let's explore these aspects of coming to know God.

Critical and Constructive

First, our task is critical in that we test various expressions
of faith by asking: Are they true? appropriate? clear? cogent?
credible? Are they based on love? Do they provide the church
and its members with a witness that is faithful to the gospel
as reflected in our living heritage and that is authentic and
convincing in the light of human experience and the present
state of human knowledge?

Our theological task is also constructive in that every
generation must appropriate creatively the wisdom of the
past and seek God in their midst in order to think afresh
about God, revelation, sin, redemption, worship, the church,
freedom, justice, moral responsibility, and other significant
theological concerns. Our summons is to understand and
receive the gospel promises in our troubled and uncertain
times.

Individual and Communal

Our theological task is also both individual and communal.
It is a feature in the ministry of individual Christians and
requires the participation of all who are in our church.
Because the mission of the church is to be carried out by
everyone who is called to discipleship, our theological task
is also communal. It unfolds in conversations open to the
experiences, insights, and traditions of all constituencies that
make up United Methodism.

Contextual and Incarnational

Next, our theological task is contextual and incarnational. It
is grounded upon God's supreme mode of self-revelation.
We understand this as the Incarnation in Jesus Christ that is
energized by our involvement in the daily life of the church
and the world, as we participate in God's liberating and
saving action.

Practical

Finally, our theological task is essentially practical. Our understanding of God should inform the individual's daily decisions and serve the life and work of the church. We should be able to "walk our talk." Therefore, as confirmation leaders, we should create an experience that offers individuals the opportunity to reflect upon God in ways that are critical and constructive, focused not only on themselves but also others, and practical so that they may feel empowered to exercise their understanding of God as they engage the church and the world.

Confirmation is an extension of the relationship that God initiates in baptism (see "What Is Confirmation?"). So it follows that God continues to act in a self-giving way through the confirmation community because of the relationship previously established. That relationship—binding and inescapable—is also known as a covenant. Covenant and community are foundational to our understanding of and participation in God's work. Let's explore each of these.

Covenant

The relationship between God and humanity, is mentioned in both the Old and New Testaments. Thanks to Jesus work on the cross, throughout biblical history, and ultimately to all of humanity, God established a new covenantal relationship that promises eternal life, grace, divine provision, and protection. This covenant shall never be broken by God because it is permanent. Unfortunately, however, the covenant has been mishandled by us throughout history. Our humanness can cause us to think more highly of ourselves than of God. Even though God intends the covenant for our good, we often reject God's faithfulness for our short-sighted thinking. As a result, such actions lead to situations that do not glorify God and lead to accountability and consequences. Instead our responsibility is to respond in obedience and to praise God for such mighty acts. Also, our responsibility is to honor the covenant so that the witness in Christ will encourage others to do the same.

Confirmation, then, is an opportunity for us to live into the covenant which God has made in such a way that each student, through the work of the Holy Spirit, will willingly embrace the covenant with a complete understanding of the commitment and responsibility required. In order for the individual to faithfully live into this covenant, we must teach in such a way that her or his heart will be led to say "yes" to Christ. Now that we have covered the meaning and importance of covenant, let us turn our attention to the importance of community.

Community

Confirmation offers a special community where intentional nurturing and faith formation can occur. As previously stated, God who is self-giving in baptism is present and extended in confirmation through the various types of community that are formed during this experience. Therefore, community is an important part of confirmation. As Jesus is teaching about how we should welcome, value, and relate to one another, he offers these words:

> *"For where two or three are gathered in my name,*
> *I'm there with them" (Matthew 18:20).*

Community matters and the community formed through each confirmation experience is precious because Jesus is in the midst—available to each person involved. We must not only remember this but also create a space that honors Jesus' presence and the possibilities that entails.

As Jesus stated, the environment should be welcoming, nonjudgmental, and encouraging so that each person feels free. It should be a safe space where the individual dares to encounter God in a new way. It should be a nurturing space where questions about that encounter are freely expressed by all. While there is a larger community formed by all who are involved, it is also important to remember that there are communities within the whole that should offer the same sense of being.

Each of the iterations of community that are possible during confirmation should be encouraged and supported. These communities are family, peer to peer, mentor/mentee, youth group, and the broader church. Each community is important because each of us encounters God in different ways, and each type provides unique opportunities through which young people encounter the self-giving of God. Therefore, even though it is not a sacrament, our view of this experience and the potential for a young person to encounter God should yield a sacramental view of confirmation.

Methodist's Theological Perspective on Confirmation

Indeed, confirmation offers young people an intentional time to explore God, but many did not believe that confirmation was necessary, including John Wesley, the founder of the Methodist movement. Wesley intentionally stressed that there were only two sacraments: baptism and Communion. He questioned the need for confirmation. Because baptism serves as the entry point for Christian community and offers regeneration to all, Wesley wondered why one would "bother with confirmation" when baptism was all-encompassing. In fact, he was so against confirmation that he did not include it in the *Book of Worship for American Methodists.*

However, Wesley did affirm the importance of the personal appropriation of that which was communicated in baptism. "He constantly reminded parents and pastors of the importance of their teaching and discipline as part of the church's role in helping its baptized members fulfill the promise in Baptism."[3] As such, there was a constant tension for him between the prevenient grace and regenerating spirit that incorporates children into the church and the need for a subsequent profession of faith which Wesley had to acknowledge.[4] Even with his beliefs regarding baptism, Wesley had to acknowledge this need for the individual to process his or her faith for salvation.

As a result of this tension, we as United Methodists have the shortest history with regard to confirmation among our brothers and sisters in other denominations. In our Methodist history, confirmation language began to appear in the early 1900s in services although not officially in our worship publications. At one time, baptized children of the church were presented as those who desired to confirm the vows of their baptism and to enter into the active duties and the full privileges of membership in Christ's church. Those who were baptized as infants/children were classified as "preparatory members" and a special service was held at the appropriate time for them. While this service was not called confirmation, the language of the Spirit's action in strengthening members was incorporated.[5]

As the Methodist Church continued to explore its identity, its way of doing confirmation varied as well. By the 1950s, the term *confirmation* was more widely used. In the 1964 *Book of Worship*, the term *confirmation* was adopted at General Conference.[6] While this was done "officially" by the church to clarify the importance of baptism in the 1960s, the Methodist Church continued to further define it. Changes to the confirmation service continued throughout the 1980s and 1990s, making it clear that confirmation pointed back to baptism.[7]

According to Richard Osmer, the new baptismal and confirmation services added a strong covenantal framework to the earlier understanding.[8] Today, in the section "Concerning The Services of the Baptismal Covenant," the words "those baptized before they are old enough to take the vows for themselves make their personal profession of faith in the service called confirmation" and distinguishes this group from "those who are able to take the vows for themselves at their baptism" who are not confirmed.[9] "No separate ritual of confirmation is needed for the believing person." [10] To be clear, confirmation is not a process offered for one to "join the church," because that actually happens during baptism. Confirmation enables individuals to respond in faith for themselves to the United Methodist tradition and commit to give their prayers, presence, gifts, witness, and service to the church. [11] But there is more to the experience than that of the individual. In addition to the individual's personal commitment to the baptismal covenant, confirmation confirms God's promise made in baptism and the congregation's commitment made in baptism.

The individual confirms the grace of God received during baptism and the covenant community confirms its joining in the growth in grace but, ultimately, confirmation is the work of the Holy Spirit. Because confirmation is understood as the strengthening of and making firm of one in Christian faith and life, it is the Holy Spirit that does the confirming. [12]

Further, because confirmation seals in covenant the personal commitment of one who was baptized into Christian community under the commitment of a parent, guardian, or sponsor, it eliminates the need to be confirmed for adults who responded in baptism for themselves. Confirmation does not bestow the Holy Spirit because that has already occurred in baptism. Thus, the Holy Spirit is already present.

Confirmation also rules out the misnomer that reaffirming baptism occurs only once. Because salvation is an ongoing process towards "Christian perfection," then the reaffirming of the baptismal covenant should be a continuous process. [13] The *United Methodist Hymnal* states that after confirmation or baptism, when candidates take vows for themselves, Christians are encouraged to reaffirm the Baptismal Covenant from time to time. This, of course, is not to be misunderstood as a re-baptism. As United Methodists we believe that "God's promise to us in the sacrament is steadfast." [14]

Given all of the changes that have occurred in the history of Christian initiation, and confirmation specifically for our purposes, it is understandable why there is often confusion about what each means and how each connect. So, let us consider the following frequently asked questions as you convey the importance of confirmation.

Practical Questions With Theological Underpinnings

As you may or may not be aware, you as the teacher/ leader will be viewed as the resident expert on "all things confirmation." However, being bestowed with such a responsibility should not cause alarm. Please know that because God's ways are mysterious, and God has not fully revealed God's self to any of us, it is not humanly possible to know all of the answers. Hebrews 11:1 reminds us:

> *"Faith is the reality of what we hope for, the proof of what we don't see."*

In fact, there will be *who*, *what*, *when*, *where*, *how*, and *why* questions to which only God knows the answers. This should be both freeing for you and for students who believe they need complete understanding.

My child is not excited about being a part of confirmation. Does he/she have to participate?

While we cannot force faith upon others, it is important for parents to understand that the commitment they made when their child was baptized is not enough for the child's salvation. When their son or daughter was baptized, the parents reaffirmed their faith and agreed to "nurture your child in Christ's holy church, that by your teaching and example they may be guided to accept God's grace for themselves, to profess their faith openly, and to lead a Christian life."[15] But each person must accept Jesus Christ as Lord and Savior personally in order for his or her faith to be understood as his or her own and truly "walk in the way that leads to life."[16]

Are adults confirmed?

Adults who are presented for baptism and respond individually do not need to be confirmed for "they have made their public profession of faith at the font" and taken their vows for him or herself.[17]

What is the purpose of adult confirmation class?

There are several scenarios where this could be an option. The first is for the parents of confirmands. In my experience of teaching confirmation, parents often realize that their child going through confirmation knows more about the United Methodist way than they do. As a result, these parents have asked for a similar class so they can learn as well. I have also had parents ask to sit in on the student classes in order to learn along with their teens—and both were welcomed enthusiastically.

Another scenario is possible for individuals coming from another faith tradition to join the church. While a new-member class is one option, some people may be seeking a more extensive learning opportunity. These individuals could join the parents of confirmands for a potentially rewarding experience.

How long should a confirmation experience last? How long does it take for the Holy Spirit to work?

Confirmation is not an event unto itself. The work of the Holy Spirit begins before that moment, continues in that moment, and extends beyond that moment because we are constantly growing, learning, and moving towards perfection. As a result,

Confirm Director Guide

there is no way of attaching a timetable to the work of the Holy Spirit.

Context should be your best guide for the most appropriate length of time for a confirmation experience. Consider the following:

• You may have one student who receives one-on-one attention for three months, during which you cover all of the necessary topics ("how to" is discussed in the next section).

• You may have a group of ten students receiving extensive instruction during Sunday school or during children's ministry activities who already know the material you will cover.

• Or, you might have a group of two hundred children who have no interest in anything related to confirmation.

Each of these scenarios requires a different amount of time. However, regardless of the situation, it is important to remember that not all can be covered in such an experience that one's faith will be complete. It is necessary that individuals continue to learn even after they are confirmed.

The Church's Role in Confirmation and the Continuum of Faith Formation

In *A Hidden Wholeness*, Parker Palmer states that there is no other group or agency that can do what the church does: make it "safe for the soul to show up and offer us its guidance."[18] As baptized children grow, they need constant and intentional nurture. If a person is to be empowered to live out faithfully the human side of the baptismal covenant, Christian nurture is essential and the responsibility belongs not only to parents but also to the entire faith community.

The church itself is a means of grace in the lives of children growing up within it; it is an instrument needed for the shaping of Christians. Christian nurture should include both the cognitive process of learning and the spiritual process of formation. Nurture should begin before the confirmand professes his or her faith and it should be ongoing.[19]

What happens during the confirmation experience?

In these weekly classes, confirmands will be exposed to the United Methodist way of faith. While openly discussing history, theological concepts, and membership in the church, we trust the Holy Spirit will be inwardly at work. In order for the confirmand to understand what it means to personally respond to Christ and then do so, each student will develop a deeper relationship with God and his or her peers, while learning about himself or herself during the confirmation experience. The teenager will learn about how important it is to be involved in the life of the church and what that involvement requires of him or her. He or she will begin to put this understanding into practice while engaging with leaders of the church, learning their gifts and graces, and finding opportunities to be engaged well after the confirmation experience concludes.

What happens after my child is confirmed?

As United Methodists we believe the ministry of all Christians in Christ's name and spirit is both a gift and a task (see ¶129 in *The Book of Discipline of the United Methodist Church*). The gift is God's unmerited grace; the task is unstinting service. Entrance into and acceptance of ministry begin in a local church, but the impulse to minister always moves one beyond the congregation toward the whole human community. God's gifts are richly diverse for a variety of services; yet all have dignity and worth. Each member commits to give their prayers, presence, gifts, witness, and service in all aspects of life as Christians (see ¶217.6 in *The Book of Discipline*).

When the confirmation experience is done well, everyone involved is transformed, including the leader, because of the encounter with God through this special community. Not only does the student cultivate a deeper level of faith to live out in The United Methodist Church and the world, but also the volunteers, mentors, parents, and the congregation are reminded of their personal faith journey. Ultimately, everyone is strengthened and the congregation is more "alive" and better able to witness to God's faithfulness as it continues to baptize and teach toward the transformation of the world.

Confirmation is an opportunity for us to live into the covenant which God has made in such a way that each student, through the work of the Holy Spirit, will willingly embrace the covenant with a complete understanding of the commitment and responsibility required.

Excerpts from The Book of Discipline of The United Methodist Church [20]

¶1104. Section 3—Our Doctrinal Standards and General Rules

THE ARTICLES OF RELIGION OF THE METHODIST CHURCH

Article I—Of Faith in the Holy Trinity

There is but one living and true God, everlasting, without body or parts, of infinite power, wisdom, and goodness; the maker and preserver of all things, both visible and invisible. And in unity of this Godhead there are three persons, of one substance, power, and eternity—the Father, the Son, and the Holy Ghost.

Article II—Of the Word, or Son of God, Who Was Made Very Man

The Son, who is the Word of the Father, the very and eternal God, of one substance with the Father, took man's nature in the womb of the blessed Virgin; so that two whole and perfect natures, that is to say, the Godhead and Manhood, were joined together in one person, never to be divided; whereof is one Christ, very God and very Man, who truly suffered, was crucified, dead, and buried, to reconcile his Father to us, and to be a sacrifice, not only for original guilt, but also for actual sins of men.

Article III—Of the Resurrection of Christ

Christ did truly rise again from the dead, and took again his body, with all things appertaining to the perfection of man's nature, wherewith he ascended into heaven, and there sitteth until he return to judge all men at the last day.

Article IV — Of the Holy Ghost

The Holy Ghost, proceeding from the Father and the Son, is of one substance, majesty, and glory with the Father and the Son, very and eternal God.

Article V — Of the Sufficiency of the Holy Scriptures for Salvation

The Holy Scripture containeth all things necessary to salvation; so that whatsoever is not read therein, nor may be proved thereby, is not to be required of any man that it should be believed as an article of faith, or be thought requisite or necessary to salvation. In the name of the Holy Scripture we do understand those canonical books of the Old and New Testament of whose authority was never any doubt in the church.

Article VIII — Of Free Will

The condition of man after the fall of Adam is such that he cannot turn and prepare himself, by his own natural strength and works, to faith, and calling upon God; wherefore we have no power to do good works, pleasant and acceptable to God, without the grace of God by Christ preventing us, that we may have a good will, and working with us, when we have that good will.

THE CONFESSION OF FAITH OF THE EVANGELICAL UNITED BRETHREN CHURCH

Article III — The Holy Spirit

We believe in the Holy Spirit who proceeds from and is one in being with the Father and the Son. He convinces the world of sin, of righteousness and of judgment. He leads men through faithful response to the gospel into the fellowship of the Church. He comforts, sustains and empowers the faithful and guides them into all truth.

Article V — The Church

We believe the Christian Church is the community of all true believers under the Lordship of Christ. We believe it is one, holy, apostolic and catholic. It is the redemptive fellowship in which the Word of God is preached by men divinely called, and the sacraments are duly administered according to Christ's own appointment. Under the discipline of the Holy Spirit the Church exists for the maintenance of worship, the edification of believers and the redemption of the world.

¶102. SECTION 1 — OUR DOCTRINAL HERITAGE

Distinctive Wesleyan Emphases

Although Wesley shared with many other Christians a belief in grace, justification, assurance, and sanctification, he combined them in a powerful manner to create distinctive emphases for living the full Christian life. The Evangelical United Brethren tradition, particularly as expressed by Phillip William Otterbein from a Reformed background, gave similar distinctive emphases.

Grace pervades our understanding of Christian faith and life. By grace we mean the undeserved, unmerited, and loving action of God in human existence through the ever-present Holy Spirit. While the grace of God is undivided, it precedes salvation as "prevenient grace," continues in "justifying grace," and is brought to fruition in "sanctifying grace."

We assert that God's grace is manifest in all creation even though suffering, violence, and evil are everywhere present. The goodness of creation is fulfilled in human beings, who are called to covenant partnership with God. God has endowed us with dignity and freedom and has summoned us to responsibility for our lives and the life of the world.

In God's self-revelation, Jesus Christ, we see the splendor of our true humanity. Even our sin, with its destructive consequences for all creation, does not alter God's intention for us—holiness and happiness of heart. Nor does it diminish our accountability for the way we live.

Despite our brokenness, we remain creatures brought into being by a just and merciful God. The restoration of God's image in our lives requires divine grace to renew our fallen nature.

Prevenient Grace—We acknowledge God's prevenient grace, the divine love that surrounds all humanity and precedes any and all of our conscious impulses. This grace prompts our first wish to please God, our first glimmer of understanding concerning God's will, and our "first slight transient conviction" of having sinned against God.

God's grace also awakens in us an earnest longing for deliverance from sin and death and moves us toward repentance and faith.

Justification and Assurance—We believe God reaches out to the repentant believer in justifying grace with accepting and pardoning love. Wesleyan theology stresses that a decisive change in the human heart can and does occur under the prompting of grace and the guidance of the Holy Spirit.

In justification we are, through faith, forgiven our sin and restored to God's favor. This righting of relationships by God through Christ calls forth our faith and trust as we experience regeneration, by which we are made new creatures in Christ.

This process of justification and new birth is often referred to as conversion. Such a change may be sudden and dramatic, or gradual and cumulative. It marks a new beginning, yet it is part of an ongoing process. Christian experience as personal transformation always expresses itself as faith working by love.

Our Wesleyan theology also embraces the scriptural promise that we can expect to receive assurance of our present salvation as the Spirit "bears witness with our spirit that we are children of God."

Sanctification and Perfection—We hold that the wonder of God's acceptance and pardon does not end God's saving work, which continues to nurture our growth in grace. Through the power of the Holy Spirit, we are enabled to increase in the knowledge and love of God and in love for our neighbor.

New birth is the first step in this process of sanctification. Sanctifying grace draws us toward the gift of Christian perfection, which Wesley described as a heart "habitually filled with the love of God and neighbor" and as "having the mind of Christ and walking as he walked."

This gracious gift of God's power and love, the hope and expectation of the faithful, is neither warranted by our efforts nor limited by our frailties.

Chapter Two Endnotes

1. Miller, Randolph Crump, ed. *Theologies of Religious Education* (Birmingham, Ala.: Religious Press, 1995); 4.

2. *The Book of Discipline of The United Methodist Church, 2012*. Copyright © 2012 by The United Methodist Publishing House; ¶105, page 78. Used by permission.

3. Richard Robert Osmer, *Confirmation: Presbyterian Practices in Ecumenical Perspective* (Louisville, Ky.: Geneva Press, 1996); 107.

4. Ibid. (See also notes on grace as a Wesleyan Emphasis on page 57 of this book.)

5. Ibid., 108.

6. Ibid., 106.

7. Ibid., 109.

8. Ibid., 110.

9. *The United Methodist Hymnal,* "Concerning the Services of the Baptismal Covenant" (Nashville, TN.: The United Methodist Publishing House, 1989); 32. Used by permission.

10. Gayle Carlton Felton, *By Water and the Spirit: Making Connections for Identity and Ministry* (Nashville, Tn.: Discipleship Resources, 1997); 37.

11. See *The Book of Discipline*, ¶217.6, page 153.

12. Felton, *By Water and the Spirit*, 37.

13. Osmer, *Confirmation: Presbyterian Practices*, 110.

14. *The United Methodist Hymnal*, 32.

15. *The United Methodist Hymnal*, Baptismal Covenant I, 34.

16. Ibid., 35.

17. *The United Methodist Hymnal*, "Concerning the Services of the Baptismal Covenant," 32.

18. Parker J. Palmer, *A Hidden Wholeness: The Journey Toward an Undivided Life* (San Francisco, CA: Jossey-Bass, 2004), 22.

19. Felton, *By Water and Spirit*, 35.

20. *The Book of Discipline*; ¶104, pages 63-65, 71; ¶102, pages 49-51.

Why Confirmation Matters

"Confirmation is a distinctive moment on an unfolding journey." [1]

As we discussed previously, confirmation is not sacramental for United Methodists, but it is significant. In this section we will explore four ways in which confirmation is significant. First, we will explore confirmation as an extension of baptism. Then, we will look at it as a form of discipleship that further connects the individual to God. Next, we will look at how it connects the individual to the church in a more meaningful way. Finally, we will consider how confirmation can strengthen the church.

An Extension of the Baptismal Covenant

Confirmation is an extension of baptism, both in word and deed. So, let us begin by considering what happens in "The Services of the Baptismal Covenant." When an infant is baptized, either a parent or sponsor responds in faith on behalf of that person. In this service, the pastor asks the adult if he or she will "nurture *these children (persons)* in Christ's holy church, that by your teaching and example they may be guided to accept God's grace for themselves, to profess their faith openly, and to lead a Christian life?" [2] The adult inevitably responds with "I do."

The pastor then asks the members of the congregation if they will "nurture one another in the Christian faith and life and include *these persons* now before you in your care?" Again, there is a resounding "I do." Then, the congregation continues its commitment by saying the following:

With God's help, we will proclaim the good news
    and live according to the example of Christ.
We will surround these persons
    with a community of love and forgiveness
    that they may grow in their trust of God,
    and be found faithful in their service to others.
We will pray for them,
    that they may be true disciples
    who walk in the way that leads to life. [3]

This is then followed by more questions of examination and thanksgiving over the water before the individuals are baptized and officially welcomed into the church. With everyone's involvement, including God as the primary agent, the covenant is sealed. Eventually the worship service ends with the sending forth. Unfortunately, however, the "surrounding" to which everyone committed does not always translate from words into action. In most congregations, the baptismal covenant is dismissed until the hymnal is opened again for the "I do" commitment to another person. Even though this has become the reality in many of our United Methodist congregations, this not what God intended for our covenantal life together.

Recently I saw this reality lived out as I witnessed the baptism of a baby girl. Alarm bells went off inside of me. No, the actual baptism did not cause alarm, because I fully believe God's grace filled that moment. However, I was alarmed by the less than faithful behavior of some who "surrounded" her, while others—only a few others—seemed to sincerely grasp the significance of the moment.

Among all who covenanted to nurture this sweet girl on that day was a large contingent of family and friends whose cameras were shuttering as fast as the devices would allow. I watched as they smiled widely, seemingly joyful about the event they were so intentional about capturing. As baptism is intended to occur in community, there was also a congregation, including myself. All of our eyes were fixed on the baby girl—or, shall I say, at least most of the congregation focused on the one who was being baptized into the body of believers on that day.

During the reading of the baptismal liturgy, a couple eagerly shared a story about a burst pipe with several members seated near them. I found the conversation both distracting and disrespectful. Amazingly, I could hear every word of their conversation even though I was sitting several rows ahead of them and on the opposite side of the aisle. I cringed as they talked. I was disturbed by their lack of awareness of the moment's significance and their distraction from it. Several questions, among other thoughts, ran through my head as their lengthy conversation continued.

I could not help but wonder if they were fully aware that a baptism was taking place while they were talking about water damage. How ironic, right? I also wondered if they were aware of their responsibility to nurture this sweet girl as a part of the community of believers. How could they respond appropriately during the liturgy when they had not been paying attention? Would they respond? Did they even care?

As I mentioned, two things caused alarm for me. As if the behavior of the members of the congregation were not appalling enough, the second situation shocked me even more. The extended family members who initially provided a great presence of witnesses left the service immediately following the baptism ritual.

Earlier a large group of individuals had entered the sanctuary. Within the first twenty minutes of the worship service, at least thirty extended family members and friends were seated behind the parents and grandmother of the baby that was to be baptized. This large group was quite noticeable, rivaling the congregation's normal Sunday morning worship attendance, which has dwindled over the years. I remember smiling because so many people were present for this special occasion—which I believed was a powerful statement of love and support.

At the moment when the baby girl was to be baptized, the pastor invited the parents and their family and friends to meet him at the altar. I recall watching row after row of people move forward. In fact, so many individuals were standing at the chancel rail that I could no longer see the pastor nor the baby. Still, I marveled at the beautiful image of the large crowd gathered at the altar in support of this baby.

After the baby was baptized, the entire congregation sang, "Yes, Jesus Loves Me." Even the people who had engaged in the sidebar conversation were singing. When the song ended, the pastor directed the family to return to their seats. At this point, the beautiful moment took a turn. I watched in shock as family member after family member dropped off a hymnal, walked past the pews, and proceeded to exit. The same family members who had just committed to help "nurture this baby in Christ's holy church by teaching and example" made a mad dash for the door. I wondered if any of them thought about the example they were providing to begin this newly established covenant.

Eventually only the mother, father, baby girl, and her grandmother remained. The quick departure of the other family members was so obvious that even the pastor noticed as he returned to the pulpit and saw the empty pews. If only he could have yelled out to them and said: "Stop! Do you not understand what just happened? Do you recall the commitment you just made?" If only I could have turned to those talking members and asked them to be quiet and pay attention! This situation raises many questions for us to explore in order to better understand how we currently live out our baptismal covenant and how we can improve our efforts. Consider the following:

- First, do we view this God-ordained sacrament as separate and apart from the worship of God who made the act possible?

• Then, we must ask ourselves if we, the family and congregation, fully understand what it means to "surround" those with whom we make covenant? Do we understand that our covenant agreement means that we are responsible for the individuals' spiritual development as they "grow in their trust in God" and "walk in the way that leads to life"?

• Furthermore, do we understand the lifelong connection between the sacraments, Sunday worship, and the church—all members of the body of believers? Are we doing damage by not taking this act of grace more seriously?[4]

Our lack of understanding of the baptismal covenant has led to a disconnect between the generations in the church, our commitment to young people, and ultimately between young people, the relevance that they are seeking for their life, and the church.

This important matter requires the church's immediate attention. It requires the church to first acknowledge its contribution to its current reality. Then the church must be intentional about offering ministry that will reclaim the young people it baptized and agreed to "surround and nurture."

According to both Kenda Dean and David Kinnaman—advocates for youth engagement in the life of the church—the church is responsible for the apathy among young people, because it lost its appreciation for younger generations over time. Also, because the church caused the apathy, then it is the responsibility of the church, not the youth, to fix this issue.[5] For Dean, the religious faith of young people, as it currently is lived out, is not durable enough to survive long after they graduate from high school, which is the fault of the church.[6]

Kinnaman supports Dean's argument in his book, *You Lost Me*. Kinnaman unapologetically declares:

> *"The Christian church in the United States has a shallow faith problem because we have a discipleship problem. Moreover, diagnosing and treating shallow faith among young people is urgent because we have a shallow faith problem among all adults."*[7]

In other words, we cannot expect the issue to improve over time. If adults do not help to disciple young people, then those same young people will become adults who will, in turn, fail to disciple the next generation of young people. For Kinnaman, this shallow faith can be attributed to a "failure to provide meaningful rituals"—or, a "failure to provide a clear sense of their meaning and importance."[8]

Confirmation matters! It has the potential to provide an opportunity to engage youth in a way that enables the Holy Spirit to "stir up" their gifts. Confirmation can potentially renew the church's commitment to covenantal relationships, build upon relationships between the various age groups, and bolster the ministry that is offered to young people. Confirmation should matter because it is a process of ritual that provides a clear sense of meaning and importance of faith and how it is lived out in The United Methodist Church.

Confirmation should be viewed not with dread but with excitement. It has the potential to serve a point of connection in the continuation of ministry with young people, as an integral stage in the discipleship. It also has the potential for renewal and vitality which is necessary for the entire church.

Let's consider the following as it relates to confirmation:

- connection and continuation,

- the potential for discipleship,

- and its impact on the vitality of the church.

Intentional Connection to God— Discipleship

"The whole process [of faith] is dynamically connected, each successive spiral stage linked to and adding to the previous ones. Each stage ... marks the rise of a new set of capacities or strength in faith." —James Fowler [9]

James Fowler also states in *Stages of Faith* that conversion,

"...from one stage to another, is a significant re-centering of one's previous conscious or unconscious images of value and power, and the conscious adoption of a new set of master stories in the commitment to reshape one's life in a new community of interpretation and action." [10]

To put it simply, the way that a sixth grader responds in faith will be different from that of a third grader and also that of a senior in high school. This person's faith should be more developed than it was in elementary school, but on a trajectory to become that of a high schooler preparing to graduate and make important life decisions. In *Confirmation*, Osmer names the purpose of confirmation as a time when the Holy Spirit strengthens the individual in faith. [11]

Confirmation is a time when individuals can explore the biblical stories learned in children's church in order to understand them more fully and also appropriate them so they become personal, relevant, and deeply meaningful. Confirmation is a time when any questions can be asked.

One year during confirmation, a student shared that he often heard the words *Alpha* and *Omega* in prayers but was not sure what they meant in terms of who God was to him. I offered a few examples of "beginning" and "end" but could see that none of them actually satisfied his curiosity. So, I grabbed a round plate from the snack table and, extending the plate, asked him to show me either the beginning or the end of the round plate. Needless to say, he could not. While it may not have been the most theological response or illustration of my career, I saw the proverbial lightbulb; the connection was made.

It is important to state up front that, as a rule, there are no "stupid questions" in the confirmation experience. It is equally important for youth to understand that, in the mystery of God, not all questions will have answers. Furthermore, I believe that just as it is important for students to feel free to express their questions and struggles, it also is critically important for the teachers, adult volunteers, and mentors to name their questions and struggles. We must remember that our founder wrestled with his faith, but then he claimed it and went on to do amazing things. Such sharing lowers the wall and allows truth to become a meeting point. Such sharing is freeing both for you and the students. This type of sharing has been commonplace throughout my journey with confirmation classes and critical to the powerful experiences we've had. A level of trust was created that allowed me to be pastor well after the confirmation experience was over.[12]

Connecting the Dots—Keeping Young People Engaged in the Church

Shifting from one sense of security to another can be challenging. For youth, a shift from what they have known to what is unfamiliar can be scary. According to Arnold van Gennep, individuals need a process to help them to negotiate transitions.[13] It is significant to note that young people do this all of the time outside of the church. They transition from kindergarten to first grade, from elementary school to middle school, from middle school to high school, from high school to college, and then from college into the real world. Our educational system has prepared them for these transitions. There are numbers of progression that represent grade levels, and subjects and increased responsibilities serve as markers for these transitions. There are also teachers, peers, and events (such as graduation) that help with these transitions.

Confirm Director Guide

In the church, however, such demarcations are not as clear. An individual will shift from the nursery to the children's ministry and then into youth ministry (maybe a mid-high school group depending on the size of the church), but the markers are not as clearly defined and the guidance is not as readily available. The two most significant transitions for young people in the church are the shift from children's ministry to youth ministry and then later from youth ministry to college level/young adult ministry. Neither are given the necessary amount of attention in the majority of our congregations. Churches must be intentional about providing the necessary markers and guidance to help young people negotiate from one stage to the next—and both should be offered during the confirmation experience.

According to van Gennep, rites of passage are helpful in these transitions. They provide a preliminal phase of separation, a liminal phase of transition, and a postliminal phase of incorporation.[14] High school graduation, for example, serves as a rite of passage. While high school graduates are normally recognized in church, that rite of passage helps to negotiate life outside of the church but does little for life beyond high school in the church. In fact, youth often attempt to return to the youth group because they seek that sense of belonging and familiarity that is missing elsewhere. Sadly, even when they realize they have outgrown the group, they stay because they have not yet learned how to negotiate "adult church" and help in such navigation is limited. Even more regretful is that this happens too often in our churches and is a major factor in why the numbers of "nones" continue to rise.

The term *none* was created by Barry Kosmin, the principle investigator for the American Religious Identity Study, and based upon responses to the open-ended question: "What is your religion, if any?" The commonality of the response "none" or "no religion" caused Kosmin to take note and eventually became the label of a generation that is disconnected from the church. This 2008 study was a replica of a study conducted in 1990 by the same academic research team using an identical methodology and the same unprompted questions.[15] Since that time the label "none" has been further defined as "nones" age and began to have families of its own. Today, "nones" are grouped into the following categories: "no way," "no longer," "never have," and "not yet." The first two groups are not at all interested in church, while the other two groups are still open to the possibility.[16] For such individuals, confirmation could be the ideal entre into church life, especially for children of "nones."

Confirmation normally happens at an important time in the life of the average young person in the church. Although there has been much debate regarding the appropriate age for confirmation, most individuals participate while in middle school, which also serves as an important time in one's developmental cycle. Confirmation should not only serve as a connecting point in the church but also strive to help young people to connect the dots between the church and other aspects of their life.

During this time students are negotiating biological, social, and spiritual transitions. They are shifting from childhood into puberty, elementary school into middle school, and also between children's and youth ministry. Confirmation is uniquely positioned to entertain the confluence of each of these transitions.[17] Done well, confirmation can provide the liminal space necessary for an individual to negotiate the transition from one way of being into another.

If we envisioned ministry with young people on a continuum of development, then we could have a greater impact on how well we disciple them. If we thought about ministry across all age groups for young people, then we could eliminate the concept of silo ministry and disjointed relationships. By changing our way of thinking, we could build covenantal relationships that would be wholistic and meet the varying needs of young people.

In my first year of full-time ministry, I served as an associate pastor with a responsibility to youth. In the first few months,

I noticed there were several ministry efforts for youth in the church that were not connected to the youth ministry program. While I was at that time, and still am, a huge proponent of variety in activities so that they appeal to the vast array of interests in young people, I believe that the various ministry activities should relate to one another. From a visioning perspective, it helps one to set and achieve goals when all who have interest in the well-being of young people operate on the same page. From a practical perspective, it helps young people to maximize their opportunity for growth. For example, a young person should not have to choose between Bible study and choir rehearsal because the two are scheduled at the same time. Not only should we collaborate in visioning, planning, and scheduling, but we also should develop a comprehensive plan for development. While this speaks directly to ministry activities in youth ministry, I believe this connectedness also should exist between children's ministry, young adult ministry, and even into adulthood. We must help individuals to connect the dots.

Let us consider the educational system in the United States that was mentioned earlier as a helper in people's transitions. There are certain requirements for each grade level. There is testing that happens in preparation for the next level, and there are also requirements that must be met before one advances.

Although no one advances through the stages of faith in exactly the same manner or according to the same time line, there are certain things a person builds upon as his or her faith develops. For example, in school one progresses from basic math to advanced math, then onward to algebra, geometry, trigonometry, and calculus. Individuals also advance in their faith. While a fifth grader can certainly have a level of faith that resembles that of an older individual, it is not the norm. What a fifth grader believes about God will be built upon as that individual asks questions, processes the answers, and internalizes them. Confirmation is a time to take what has been learned in children's ministry, family experiences, and society and develop a more advanced view of it after processing for personal relevance.

It is important to acknowledge that not all students will have grown up in the church. While the particulars about the dynamics of teaching students with various levels of understanding will be covered in the next section, I believe it is important to note that confirmation can be a significant time for those with prior knowledge as well as for those who have not yet developed that understanding.

Strengthening of the Church

Although Methodism is steeped in a rich tradition that once attracted many members, it currently faces a decline similar to that of other Protestant denominations. Today there is a disconnect between the church and the young people that it promised to "surround in love." As we explore confirmation and consider the decreasing numbers of young people who are willing to commit to the church, we must ponder the question: *Who will the church confirm if youth are not interested?* This is an alarming question considering that young people once had a significant impact on the church. Still, I do not believe that all is lost. Young people certainly have the potential. The church simply needs to give serious consideration to nurturing it.

The church can reconnect to young people by recommitting to the promises that it made during baptism. Confirmation is an opportunity for the church to reengage with young people so that they commit for themselves to that which their parents/guardians did on their behalf when they were infants. In this section we will consider the impact that young people once had on the church as a means for bolstering our desire to disciple in a way that youth today can do the same.

After all, our Methodist tradition is widely known for its emphasis on grace, social holiness, the sacraments, and discipleship. As I traced the history of this movement, I found evidence of all of these. I also found evidence of a cadre of young people whose actions helped to guide the path that has led to Methodism as we know it today, as reflected in the chart on page 76.[18]

It is important to note, however, that the Methodist tradition reaches farther into history than the 1700s in England. In fact, its roots are found in the faithfulness of two young people—Mary, who was barely a teenager when she was chosen by God for the virgin birth, and Jesus, her Son. Of the utmost significance to our faith tradition are the actions of Jesus who, as a preteen, committed to carrying out his Father's work (see Luke 2:49) and then, as a young adult, emptied himself on the cross for the salvation of humanity. Through the faithful actions of these young people, the foundation of Christianity was laid and the example for others to follow was set.

Since then there have been other heroic young people who played a significant part in the history of Christianity. In fact, Martin Luther was integral in the establishment of Protestantism, and John Wesley was integral in the establishment of Methodism at the ages of thirty-four and thirty-five, respectively. Still, the impact of young people did not end there.

A litany of young people helped to establish Methodism in America. Francis Asbury, Harry Hosier, Barbara Heck, Jarena Lee, Phoebe Palmer, and Sojourner Truth all had a significant impact on this faith tradition before they reached the age of thirty-five. While it is important to celebrate these accomplishments, it must be noted that none of these young people acted alone. Without a doubt there were others who nurtured and helped guide them. Mary had the support of Elizabeth and Joseph, among others, and Jesus had the support of many, including the disciples and John, who "prepared the way."

Comparing the role of young people in the history of the church to the role of young people in the church today, I noticed a significant shift. This stark contrast caused me to wonder:

- If young people have historically led the church forward, then what change can the church hope for if young people are not leading in a similar way today?

Furthermore, I wondered:

- Whose support do our young people have?

- Do we believe that those who sit in our confirmation classes have the potential to move the church of Jesus Christ forward?

- If we do not nurture our preteenagers and teenagers to become faithful leaders, then how can we expect them to "magically" become young adults who transform the world?

- Finally, I wondered, How can confirmation become the vehicle that helps the church reconnect with young people today?

As we consider these reasons, we must also consider what *The Book of Discipline* states about why confirmation matters: Ministry as Gift and Task states that the "ministry of all Christians in Christ's name and spirit is both a gift and a task." The gift is God's unmerited grace; the task is unstinting service. Entrance into the church is acknowledged in baptism and may include persons of all ages. In baptism, water is administered in the name of the triune God (specified in the ritual as Father, Son, and Holy Spirit) by an authorized person, and the Holy Spirit is invoked with the laying on of hands, ordinarily in the presence of the congregation. In this sacrament the church claims God's promise and the seal of the Spirit:

> *"You too heard the word of truth in Christ, which*
> *is the good news of your salvation. You were sealed*
> *with the promised Holy Spirit because you believed in*
> *Christ."—Ephesians 1:13.*

Baptism is followed by nurture and the consequent awareness by the baptized of the claim to ministry in Christ placed upon their lives by the church. Such a ministry is confirmed by the church when the pledges of baptism are accepted through profession of faith and renewed for life and mission."

The Book of Discipline also speaks to the importance of the church-school superintendent and small-group coordinator who shall be responsible for "helping to organize and supervise the total program for nurturing faith, building Christian community, and equipping people of all ages for ministry in daily life through small groups in the church."[19]

With an understanding of why confirmation matters and the inspiration to make it meaningful, pastors, teachers, parents, adult volunteers, and mentors have within their grasp an opportunity to do something amazing. Confirmation, done well, could change the way that we do church. Confirmation could change a culture through a generation of young people who had an encounter with God during their confirmation experience.

Confirmation should not only serve as a connecting point in the church but also strive to help young people to connect the dots between the church and other aspects of their life.

THE IMPACT OF YOUTH IN THE HISTORY OF CHRISTIANITY AND METHODISM

Person/Date of Birth	Moment and Year of Greatest Impact	Age
Martin Luther 1483	Protestantism, 1517	34
John Wesley 1703	Conversion, Ministry apart from Moravians, 1738	35
Barbara Heck 1734	Mother of American Methodism (changed wayward church culture), 1765	31
Francis Asbury 1745	Began preaching as teen; volunteered to come to America, 1771; named co-superintendent, 1784	26 39
Henry Hosier 1750	First Black preacher to give sermon to white audience; impacted anti-slavery movement, 1784	39
Jarena Lee 1783	Authorized to preach by Richard Allen, 1819; Ordained posthumously July 2016,	36
Sojourner Truth 1797	Won freedom for son; co-founder of Methodist church in New York, 1828	36
Phoebe Palmer 1807	Mother of Holiness Movement, 1835	28

Chapter Three Endnotes

1. Richard Robert Osmer, *Confirmation: Presbyterian Practices in Ecumenical Perspective* (Louisville, Ky.: Geneva Press, 1996); 169.
2. *The United Methodist Hymnal*, Baptismal Covenant I, "Renunciation of Sin and Profession of Faith" (Nashville, TN.: The United Methodist Publishing House, 1989); 34.
3. Ibid., 35.
4. This baptismal scenario was included in my Doctor of Educational Ministry dissertation, "Connecting the Dots Through Grace: Reclaiming What Has Been Lost," Columbia Theological Seminary, May 2016.
5. See Kenda Dean, *Almost Christian: What the Faith of Our Teenagers Is Telling the American Church* (Oxford: Oxford University Press, 2010); 3. David Kinnaman and Aly Hawkins, *You Lost Me: Why Young Christians are Leaving Church—and Rethinking Faith* (Grand Rapids, MI.: Baker Books, 2011); 12.
6. Dean, *Almost Christian*, 3.
7. David Kinnaman, and Aly Hawkins, *You Lost Me: Why Young Christians Are Leaving Church . . . and Rethinking Faith* (Grand Rapids, Mich.: Baker Books, 2011), 120.
8. Kinnaman and Hawkins, *You Lost Me*, 122.
9. James W. Fowler, *Stages of Faith: The Psychology of Human Development and the Quest for Meaning* (San Francisco: Harper Collins); 274.
10. Ibid., 282.
11. Osmer, *Confirmation: Presbyterian Practices*, 108.
12. Parker Palmer states that "teaching is always done at the dangerous intersection of personal and public life" in *The Courage to Teach: Exploring the Inner Landscape of a Teacher's Life* (San Francisco: Josey-Bass, 2007); 18.
13. Arnold van Gennep, *The Rites of Passage* (Chicago: The University of Chicago Press, 1960); 11.
14. Ibid.
15. Barry Kosmin et al., "The American Nones: The Profile of the No Religion Population," Trinity College (2008): *http://commons.trincoll.edu/aris/files/2011/08/NONES_08.pdf*. Accessed 2 April 2016.
16. Jana Blazek, "Four Kinds of 'nones'"; Lillian Daniels speaks at ACPE, *The Presbyterian Outlook*: *http://pres-outlook.org/2016/01/four-kinds-of-nones-lillian-daniel-speaks-at-apce*. Accessed 29 February 2016.
17. Most schools do not offer opportunity to explore faith because of separation between church and state; see First Amendment of the US Constitution.
18. These young people had a significant impact on the church at a young age. Some became Christian at a young age, while others were converted along the way. Yet, all of them acted on behalf of their faith in Jesus Christ. From Doctor of Educational Ministry dissertation, "Connecting the Dots Through Grace: Reclaiming What Has Been Lost," Columbia Theological Seminary, May 2016.
19. *The Book of Discipline of The United Methodist Church*, 2012. Copyright © 2012 by The United Methodist Publishing House; ¶129, page 95; ¶255, page 181. Used by permission.

Creating a Meaningful Confirmation Experience

While other groups and communities are worthy purposes, "none of them has the singular intent of a circle of trust: to make it safe for the soul to show up and offer us its guidance."—Parker Palmer [1]

"So, brothers and sisters, because of God's mercies, I encourage you to present your bodies as a living sacrifice that is holy and pleasing to God. This is your appropriate priestly service. Don't be conformed to the patterns of this world, but be transformed by the renewing of your minds so that you can figure out what God's will is—what is good and pleasing and mature." —Romans 12:1-2

"The primary purpose of teaching is to make God known."—Randolph Crump Miller [2]

"So let's continually offer up a sacrifice of praise through him, which is the fruit from our lips that confess his name. Don't forget to do good and to share what you have because God is pleased with these kinds of sacrifices." —Hebrews 13:15-16

Before talking about history, theology, *The Book of Discipline*, the importance of faith, and the commitment to the church and expectations, I spend the first session of confirmation talking about favorites—their favorites and mine. To begin, each person receives a piece of paper with a place for him or her to record the name of each person in the class. Beside each name, I include spaces for them to also record the favorite color, food, and television show as each of their peers shares. This is the ultimate icebreaker. It serves as an opportunity for teens to feel included, to connect with others, and to calm their nerves as they discover things they share in common. It is also a guarantee for laughs and side stories that lead to even more laughs. Amazingly, it also engages the student sitting in the back of the room who has little interest in being there.

To build community, I also join in the fun. Usually I share my favorite thing to eat—which always prompts a few disgusting looks and at least one "yuck!" By sharing that my favorite food to eat is vanilla ice cream and sour cream potato chips, I become real to them—well, weird and real. One year a student returned to class the following week and, during our check-in time, informed everyone that she had tried my snack and discovered that it was "actually pretty good!" She named it Ruffles Ice Cream (no connection to any actual product).

I realize this exercise may seem odd, but it is a great way to kick off the session. I always begin because it is the best way to build trust, which is my primary goal. I believe that once young people trust me enough to try a concoction like ice cream and potato chips, then they are open to hear what I say about Jesus and faith.

In the book *A Hidden Wholeness*, Parker Palmer, a noted author who places emphasis on issues in education, community, and spirituality, talks about circles of trust (small groups) and why they matter. In his book, he states that gathering in circles began in ancient times. But today there are many types of circles. There are circles whose purpose is to help individuals improve communication, resolve conflict, explore emotions, engage around a common cause, and even to further education. However, Palmer suggests that while all of these are worthy purposes, none of them has the single intent to make it safe for the soul to open up.[3]

For Palmer, a circle of trust that nurtures the soul is one that is rooted in two beliefs.

- First, the soul has "an inner teacher whose guidance is more reliable than anything we can get from doctrine, ideology, collective belief system, institution, or leader.

- "Second, we all need other people to invite, amplify, and help us discern the inner teacher's voice."[4]

Establishing the confirmation experience is the primary goal because it becomes a safe space where wonder, connection with God, and faith formation can happen through the work of the Holy Spirit. Thus far, we have discussed three essential and important elements for any confirmation experience:

- Trust

- Community

- The Holy Spirit

All other components build upon these essentials. Now we will cover the following:

- expectations and outcomes,

- engagement and involvement of all who are a part of the confirmation experience,

- the cycle of confirmation,

- the importance of personalizing the experience for each student,

- the importance of expanding the experience beyond the curriculum.

Expectations and Outcomes

Your approach to confirmation as the teacher/leader will help to foster each of these essential components; your approach to ministry will lay a foundation—good or bad. So, let's reflect upon several additional questions:

- What are your expectations for the confirmation experience?

- What type of environment do you hope to create?

- What are your goals and expectations for all who will be involved—parents, volunteers, mentors, clergy, staff, the youth group, the church, yourself, and, of course, the students?

Parker Palmer says in *A Hidden Wholeness*:

> *"Bad teachers distance themselves from the subject they are teaching—and, in the process, from their students. Good teachers join self, and subject, and students in the fabric of life. Good teachers possess a capacity for connectedness. They are able to weave a complex web of connections among themselves, their subjects, and their students so that students can learn to weave a world for themselves."* [5]

One of the blessings of being involved in the various aspects of ministry along the continuum with young people is that the blessing of growth experienced from confirmation continues long after the experience has ended. One year our youth group took a trip. The trip was an end of the year celebration, but it included a spiritual component. The students had to share their faith with strangers while visiting a theme park. They were given twenty-five wrist bands (per student) in cool colors that simply said: *Jesus loves you.* In groups, along with a chaperone, students were required to give away all the wrist bands before they could enjoy the park. Initially, they were apprehensive. However, as they began to receive smiles and other favorable responses from the people with whom they shared Jesus' love, the assignment actually became fun. It was an experience to behold!

However, that event was not the climax. Throughout the day, I interacted with several of the groups. It was all fun and games until one of the groups invited me to ride the roller coaster with them. My heart sank as I stood in front of the monstrosity. It was 3,700 feet of upside-down rolls, vertical loops, and corkscrews. It appeared to reach the heavens, and it scoured the depths several times during the ninety-second experience.

As I stood there filled with dread, one of my students said: "Pastor Tonya, you have taught us about faith. So, where is your faith? You will be OK, trust us." Well, how can you say no after that. This same young man rode with me to make sure I would be OK. As they strapped me in, he could see the terror on my face. So, he yelled out that if I screamed throughout the ride, all would be fine. No sooner had he said those words, we were off—and I was screaming! For one minute and thirty seconds, I screamed. I was jittery for a while after the ride ended, and I was hoarse for the next week, but my level of faith deepened as I learned from one of the youth.

What I had given him in the confirmation experience was reciprocated as he witnessed to me. Not only did he encourage me but also he "experienced it with me" and instructed me in helpful ways. This is what the confirmation experience should be about. In order for teens to share their faith, confirmation should be engaging, encouraging, and educational. Furthermore, as much as it is an experience for them, it should also be a formational experience for you.

Engagement and Involvement

Confirmation is an experience with many moving parts. Although short-lived, there is an intentional community formed whose purpose is aimed at the affirmative responses of the students who are involved. Because this involves different people in different ways for different reasons, preparation is important. The better equipped the members of this community are, and the more clearly these same individuals understand their role, the better the experience will be for everyone. The teacher/leader is key in this process.

This section provides a broad description for the role of the teacher in relationship to the parent, volunteer, mentor, senior pastor, other church leaders, district superintendent, former students, and the general church. While it is understood that context will augment this description, there are also some things that should be common from one church environment to the next.

Teacher

Our task is to help reclaim the excitement and intentionality that once fueled the church. Because of the changes that have occurred in our churches and society over time, I believe that confirmation is needed today as much, if not more than ever before — especially among young people who are seeking a place where they can discover meaning and purpose for their lives.

In order to reclaim that excitement, teachers must first understand what confirmation means for a young person as a way of discipleship as well as what it means to the ministry of the church as a way of encouraging faithful members. Teachers also must consider how best to convey this understanding in a way that is engaging, encouraging, and educational.

"Deep understanding is the central goal as we strive to inculcate understanding of what ... is considered true or false." [6]

To teach for understanding, teachers themselves must be comfortable with and understand the material. "Teachers need to feel expert, and they need to embody expertise in the eyes of their students. That is why young musicians love to watch their teachers perform, and tennis students want to play with their instructors." [7]

"From day one, teachers must seek to motivate their students, even against the odds. And their own belief in the importance and the rightness of what they are doing can be a pivotal motivator." —Howard Gardner [8]

In addition to your role as teacher, your vision casting, development of the experience, conveyance of the vision plan development, and execution of the plan will be key. (Later in the chapter we'll discuss the cycle of confirmation.)

If you are a first-time leader, this task may seem intimidating. However, seek guidance from the senior pastor, a former teacher, or even an expert from another church in your district or conference. They will be more than willing to help and guide you.

If you have been teaching for a while, it is always helpful to reflect upon previous experiences and evaluate what you might do better. It's also a great idea to talk to leaders in the area of children's ministry to learn about the students entering whom you don't know. Regardless of your level of experience, remember that teaching is a high calling and your willingness to lead is a special gift in which you will be blessed as you graciously bless others.

Parent

This group is extremely important to the overall process and requires special attention because there are so many dynamics to juggle. First, in today's society not all parenting occurs in a single-family household. Because of divorce, long-distance marriages, and other iterations, a student's attendance and experience can be complicated. Regardless of the living situations, the parents, who are the students' primary means of transportation, may not be regular weekly worship attendees. In addition, parents may be so overloaded with work or extracurricular activities for the entire family that they may be difficult to engage. Also, because some parents may not fully understand confirmation, they may be completely dismissive of the experience.

That is where your giftedness comes into play. By incorporating parents prior to the beginning of confirmation with an information session to explain the process, distribute and walk through companion resources, and reiterate the connection between baptism and confirmation, you will gain their attention. Just remember to maintain constant contact. Whether you utilize e-mail, texting, or a newsletter, provide weekly, updated information. Consider including facts from the lessons or God-moments from the experience (without using the students' names, of course). It's also a good idea to go the extra mile with "thank you's" and acknowledgments for parents who volunteer. Everyone loves a pat on the back and such acknowledgments may encourage other parents to participate.

At the very least, an informed parent might mention the "Wesleyan Quadrilateral" while stuck in traffic with a child. Building these relationships during confirmation will be key to maintaining long-term relationships in youth ministry. By impacting their child, they will be more likely to say "yes" to future requests. Because this is time-consuming, you may be tempted to hand off this role to someone else. I encourage you to follow through on this task yourself, as it will "pay dividends" in the days ahead.

Volunteer

Volunteers are key to both your sanity and your success. They are helpful to make last-minute copies, plan and help chaperone any excursions, and be available in the classroom as another set of hands and another voice of reason. The "to do" list for confirmation is long and requires people with different types of giftedness and different levels of engagement. These individuals should be committed, have a working knowledge of confirmation, and also a love for the faith formation of young people in general.

The primary goal is to enlist a cadre of dependable individuals so that you do not have to "do everything." It's important to view them and treat them as members of your team. In every sport there are players on the sidelines waiting to be called in at any time. You should think of your team in a similar way. Yes, I understand that ministry with youth does not always mean there will be plethora of volunteers "hanging around," but confirmation is a great time to begin to build this group. You may have only two volunteers in your first year, but that number will increase as you progress from year to year.

Plan a gathering for this group before confirmation begins and also before you meet with the parents. In fact, train your volunteers first and have them attend when you meet with the parents. As you prepare for their training, it is important to remember a few things. First, adults may shy away from young people because they are unclear of how to relate them. Secondly, adults do not like to feel as if their abilities are not being utilized and they are wasting their time. So, have a plan for their inclusion and be very clear about their role and your appreciation of their time.

While the volunteer role may not be the best place for the parent of a current confirmand to jump in, there may be a special opportunity at some point where a parent who really wants to be involved can assist in some way. Volunteers are key. They provide a great witness to the students. Not only does their presence convey the importance/need of volunteering but also it speaks volumes about how much the church cares about and values them as confirmands.

Mentors

I separate this role from that of other volunteers because this role is a very specific one. Not *more* important—but important in a different way. This person provides an additional layer of personalization that will extend beyond the classroom. Mentoring is more than a classroom experience. Mentors can help students to work through their beliefs and confusion in follow-up conversations that occur outside of the church. These relationships could be so involved that the mentor/ mentee may share in activities and family outings as a means of getting to know one another. Some mentors are willing to go the extra mile, while others will be willing to commit only to the required time and expectations. Either is fine. Try to get a feel for a volunteer's personality and ability to commit before you assign them to a specific student.

Being a confirmation mentor requires many of the same qualities as the teacher/leader, such as:

- Understanding of the importance confirmation,

- A passion for engagement,

- Openness to share and listen,

- An ability to relate to young people.

Training and lots of preplanning are necessary as well. Mentor training should be scheduled along with safe sanctuaries training, inclusive of background checks. It is also beneficial to provide a joint meeting of parents, mentors, and students so that everyone is clear on expectations, as boundaries and bonds are formed.

Clergy/Senior Pastor

Involve the senior pastor in confirmation as often as possible. Look for ways to include him or her and any other clergy as you think appropriate. The greater the number of opportunities for him or her to engage the group, the better the connection with the students. It also teaches students that their pastor is accessible. Offer opportunities for your clergy staff to lead discussions, especially theology and the sacraments, and to share their call story and the joys of ministry. In the event that the senior pastor's schedule is too busy for inclusion, provide frequent updates about what is going on in the classroom. Who knows—those updates may motivate him or her to stop in one day!

As you journey through confirmation, you may identify students who have a call, or some special interest or gift. In the event that you do, always share such news with your pastoral staff.

District Superintendent

It is not always an easy feat to include the district superintendents in confirmation because they are so incredibly busy; but it is a nice addition, if possible. There have been times when the DS was visiting our church during the time confirmation was in session. I always invited him to stop in and say hello and to share any words of wisdom. (Both of my district superintendents were male.)

I also invited the DS to participate in the confirmation ceremony. Remarkably, he always said yes, which made the experience even more special for the confirmands. In our connectional system, you never know when a student may have the opportunity to draw upon such an experience—an ordination service, a conference level meeting/event, or the need for a letter of recommendation.

Church Leaders

Spotlight a church ministry each week/month depending on how many ministries there are and how long the confirmation experience will last. It is a great way for students to understand how the church operates, as well as a way for them to identify places to connect and leaders who can help to make that happen.

Spotlighting ministries can also prompt guest committees or ministries to sponsor breakfast or snacks for youth. Depending on the leader, this could range from fruit, to cookies and juice, to a breakfast casserole. I have yet to meet a student who passed on a delectable treat.

As a side note, allow students to ask each "guest" to share their favorites (as described earlier), as youth add to their individual lists started at the beginning of the experience. It keeps the fun going and deepens the connections that will be important once confirmation concludes.

The Returning Student (Youth Volunteer)

On occasion there may be a former confirmand who wants to return the following year. While one school of thought argues against this, I welcome it within certain parameters. I encourage returns for sharing their confirmation experience with current students, to make announcements about upcoming youth ministry activities, or to perform specific tasks. I, however, do not allow them to come and simply hang out as an escape from other activities. I encourage them to engage in the church in new ways. If they are finding that engagement to be challenging, I enlist the help of their previous mentor to help them find their new place.

Beyond the Lessons

Rounding out the confirmation experience is always a good idea. Offering a change in scenery will allow the group to bond in a different way and the space to encounter everything in a new setting and environment. It also will allow you the opportunity to experience students outside of the classroom.

Every year our confirmation class went on a weekend get-a-way. This was always a treat. I could never determine who was happier about the weekend—the students or the parents. It was anticipated by everyone, including myself. During this weekend the most amazing things happened—the students were free to have fun, meet other confirmation students from around the conference, and engage with the community in a personal way. No matter the weather, the number of students, or the number of goofy moments, the group dynamics changed by the time we returned from the weekend. The youth were closer to one another, to the adults, and to me.

If your annual conference does not have a planned confirmation retreat, consider partnering with another church or organize and plan your own. While there are many parts of confirmation that students enjoy, the weekend retreat ranks in their Top 5 list of highlights.

Still, a retreat is not the only way to engage students. As they learn about coming of age in their tradition, it would be helpful to expose them to the process in other faith traditions. Perhaps visiting a confirmation class in the Catholic tradition, or a Bar/Bat Mitzvah in a synagogue would be meaningful. If a coming-of-age ceremony is not an option, perhaps the students could attend a service at a Greek Orthodox church. The idea is to expand their knowledge because the opportunity to experience other traditions will likely not happen outside of confirmation.

There may also be related exhibits, films, or other events pertinent to the type of experience that you aim to offer. Consider inviting professors from a local college or university who would be willing to visit your class and discuss ancient geography, languages, cultures, and so on that could bring the lessons to life.

The curriculum and the weekly lessons will be thorough and chock full of suggestions, but there may be something you could add that would enhance your experience in your particular context. The broader the experiences you choose to incorporate, the greater your ability will be to reach your students.

Everyone learns differently, and you will have different types of students and learning styles in your class. Engaging each of them will be both necessary and important in order to achieve the outcomes for which you hope and plan.

Making the Experience Personal

Different Patterns of Intelligence

According to Howard Gardner, all human beings pose at least eight separate forms of intelligence; each of which is represented in a certain part of the brain and reflects the "potential to solve problems or to fashion products that are valued in one or more cultural settings."[9] They are as follows:

- Linguistic

- Logical mathematical

- Spatial

- Musical

- Naturalistic

- Bodily kinesthetic

- Intrapersonal

- Interpersonal [10] (see pages 108-109).

While no one intelligence is better than another, each of these intelligences tap into a different area of the brain and require different methods for access. For example, a student with a musical capacity will lean into a lesson on the meaning of the hymns created by Charles Wesley, while a student with a bodily kinesthetic intelligence would appreciate being involved in the acting out of a conversation between John and Charles Wesley about said songs.

For this reason, when the different types are in the same learning environment, different approaches to learning are required. Gardner classifies these as "entry points." For him, understanding the theory of multiple intelligences can be a powerful partner in effective teaching in three ways: providing powerful entry points, offering apt analogies, and providing multiple representations of the central and core ideas of the topic. [11]

One of the videos I often us to enhance the lesson about the Beginnings of American Methodism is *Clay Ride: A Gallup Through Methodist History*. [12] By the time the students see the video, they already have read about the history and we have discussed it in class. This third iteration of the same information takes the words that have been read and spoken and conveys the message in a different way. This video was shown at a recent annual conference. While the video was playing, one of my former confirmands, a youth delegate, sent me a text to tell me that he remembered the video and the lesson. There are many types of entry points to make analogies and represent central concepts. Songs, art, other videos, life experiences, and opportunities to "act out" concepts are all ways to enhance a lesson. One way to do that weekly is to create a different type of prayer experience to begin or end the class. This could be a great augment to the class and a way to reach each of the different intelligence types. [13]

The paper plate was perhaps not the most theological explanation for God as the "Alpha and Omega," but it helped drive home the point for that student. Mentioning these eight forms of intelligence is not intended to suggest that you include eight different experiences for each lesson. It is intended to help you be more mindful of the need for variety over the course of the experience.

Making Space for Everyone

I once had a student in my class with special needs. He was mainstreamed, but required an extra step. Rather than calling attention to this student's needs, I created a fill-in-the-blank handout for the entire class (see pages 110-111). As I talked, they paid attention and filled in the blanks as needed. While this could have impacted the momentum of the class, the handout was welcomed by all. Rather than focusing on taking notes, they listened and noted the important information. This allowed additional opportunities for impromptu questions and experiences.

Feeding Their interests and Passion

In line with our understanding of the different intelligences, the students also will have different interests. Some will be very intentional about their learning and ask for additional information, books, or Scripture verses that relate to their topic of interests. Once I engaged a young lady in the Book of Revelation because she wanted to know more about what heaven would be like. I admit that she was exceptional, but there were also others who asked more probing questions.

In the past I've made it a point to tell the students that, in many ways, our Methodist history lines up with our history as Americans. Even though I provided a handout detailing the comparison, one particular young man wanted me to recommend additional resources to read because he loved history. Instances like these are precious and a pleasure for me. I never seek them, but I make it clear that no question is off limits and no wonder is unworthy of exploration.

Preparing for "No" or "Not Yet"

While you will pour yourself completely into the confirmation experience, it is important to note that a "yes" is not a guarantee for every student. Therefore, it is also important to note that it is very much OK for a student to say "no" or "not yet." Just remember that such a response is not an indictment against you or your ministry. In fact, it could be viewed favorable—that you did such a thorough job in conveying the importance of saying yes to Christ that the student understands its seriousness and therefore wants to wait in order to be fully committed to the responsibilities.

While the student's parents may view this as an embarrassment or a failure, you can help them to realize that such a sign of maturity and self-awareness should be commended and encouraged rather than viewed as a problem to be resolved. After all, we trust that the Holy Spirit is at work in that moment, right? Further, you could/should avail yourself to the individual, mentor, and family for continued nurture and exploration. Ultimately, such a serious take on the commitment that is met by graciousness could lead to a deeper faith in the long term.

Establishing the confirmation experience is the primary goal because it becomes a safe space where wonder, connection with God, and faith formation can happen through the work of the Holy Spirit.

Chapter Four Endnotes

1. Parker J. Palmer, *A Hidden Wholeness: The Journey Toward an Undivided Life* (San Francisco, CA.: Jossey-Bass, 2004); 22.
2. Randolph Crump Miller, ed., *Theologies of Religious Education* (Birmingham, AL.: Religious Education Press, 1995); 5.
3. Palmer, *Hidden Wholeness*, 22.
4. Ibid., 25, 26
5. Ibid., 25, 26
6. Howard Gardner, *The Disciplined Mind: Beyond Facts and Standardized Tests, the K-12 Education That Every Child Deserves* (New York: Penguin Books, 2000); 186.
7. Ibid., 133.
8. Ibid., 134.
9. Ibid., 71-22.
10. Ibid., 72.
11. Ibid., 187.
12. *http://shop.umc.org/clayride-a-gallop-through-methodist-history*. Accessed 27 September 2016.
13. *Imaginative Prayer for Youth Ministry* by Jeannie Oestreicher and Larry Warner could be a great resource.

Appendixes

Table of Contents

Appendix 1

Timeline for Confirmation Cycle

• Assess the outcome of the confirmation experience just completed.

    o What worked well? What did not work well?

    o What needs to change, be updated, or deleted?

    o What needs to be added?

• Review your budget and actual expenses for the completed experience.

• If there were students who were not ready to be confirmed, organize a follow-up plan.

    o Decide when you will reach out.

    o Decide who will be involved in the discussion.

    o Decide how long your follow-up process will last.

    o Decide if/how the mentor will continue to engage with the student.

• If yes, do you want frequent updates?

Confirm Director Guide

- If yes, then how often will that person update you?

- Set the dates for next year's experience and add to the church calendar.

    o Begin to invite speakers based on the timeline of topics.

    o Begin to invite ministry leaders.

    o Book any locations that require reservations.

- Create a new budget for the coming year.

- Set the dates for training sessions and information sessions. Add those dates to the church calendar.

- Begin to announce the dates and registration for the upcoming confirmation experience.

- Identify volunteers for the upcoming year.

- Set up a training session for volunteers (new and returning).

    o Make sure this happens in a timely fashion so that background checks can be completed before confirmation begins.

    o Order any materials for this session.

    o Review their roles and responsibilities for updates and changes.

    o Include Safe Sanctuaries training.

• Set up a training session for mentors (new and returning).

   o Make sure this happens in a timely fashion so that background checks can be completed before confirmation begins.

   o Order any materials needed for this session.

   o Review their roles and responsibilities for updates and changes.

   o Include Safe Sanctuaries training.

• Begin to communicate with parents about registration deadlines, the information session, and any costs or additional items that will be required at the beginning of confirmation.

   o In addition to upfront costs, it will be helpful for parents to understand exactly how much money will be required for the entire experience.

   o It is highly encouraged to hold one information session so the community-building process can begin. If this session is announced far enough in advance, higher levels of participation will be more likely.

• Meet with the Children's Director/Minister and begin to learn about students and any needs that may require special attention.

• Get to know the incoming class while they are still involved in children's ministry.

• Extend a personal invitation to each student. Have fun with this step; it can be a great beginning point!

• Meet with the senior pastor to review the previous year and to update him/her on plans for the upcoming experience.

• Meet with youth ministry team to identify ways of improving the confirmation experience based on their feedback; also identify ways to engage them with the new group once confirmation begins.

• Meet with church leaders to schedule individuals' time with the confirmation class, the topic for discussion, and their willingness to provide snacks.

• Begin a countdown plan to confirmation. Keep key volunteers informed so they can step in at any time.

  o Double check lessons weekly; check planned guest speakers, additional resources, and supplies as necessary.

• If you will be traveling with students, prepare and obtain a signed permission slip from each parent early. This should include all pertinent information necessary in an emergency—contact name and number, medications, and insurance information.

  o *Warning*: Not every parent will want you to keep such information on file, even knowing its in a secure location. Some will want to complete a new form each time.

• Ask students to complete an agreement form as well stating that they will study and take the confirmation class seriously. Also, include an agreement to Christian conduct (as you feel led to define this) in all aspects of their life, especially when on church trips.

• Meet with parents in order to review the calendar, costs, and expectations. Students may or may not be present for the parents' meeting.

• Meet with students to discuss the how and why of confirmation.

  o Parents should be present for this meeting.

o Invite a former student to share about their confirmation experience.

o This meeting should be high-energy and engaging. Videos or pictures from previous years would be a great backdrop. An example of a typical class, or even footage from a field trip, are great additions.

• Include ample lead time for announcing the upcoming confirmation experience to generate excitement and engage the entire congregation.

• Provide weekly updates to the parents after confirmation begins.

• Provide weekly updates to the senior pastor after confirmation begins.

• Provide weekly updates to the mentors and volunteers after confirmation begins.

• Send thank-you notes to volunteers who go above and beyond as necessary.

• Send notes of encouragement to students over the course of the year. By the end of confirmation, each student should have received a note from you.

• Invite the youth pastor/director/leader to be a part of the confirmation experience so they can get to know the students and share in the experience.

• Begin to plan the confirmation service.

• Begin to plan the confirmation celebration.

o Hold off on planning until you determine the personality of the class/students. This may take a few weeks, but the celebration should not only reflect them but also involve them.

o Will there be a speaker?

• Once you have a feel for the group and have a few ideas, form a confirmation celebration committee of students, parents, mentors, and other volunteers.

• Assess and reassess the confirmation experience throughout the year. Never be tied to what happened in a previous year. Allow the Holy Spirit to lead you.

• Pray daily for the students. If you have a great team of volunteers, enlist them early on in this process or offer it as an opportunity for the larger congregation. The latter would make Confirmation Sunday more meaningful to the entire congregation.

• Create new ways every year to say "thank you" to mentors and volunteers. Be personal and involve the students. Their touch will make it more creative and meaningful.

• Have fun! Trust God and enjoy the blessing!

• After the confirmation celebration and service are over, rest! Then, circle back to the parents and students as you continue to build upon the relationships you have established.

 o Offer parents ways to be involved in future confirmation classes or in youth ministry activities.

 o Make sure the students are living into their commitment by getting involved.

• Keep the mentor in the loop or make connections with other church leaders who may be helpful.

• Encourage students to become involved in district and other conference-level activities. United Methodists are a connection body with lots to offer.

• Involve the youth pastor/director/leader to make sure the continuum continues.

• **Assess the year and begin planning for the incoming group.**

• **Reflect upon your personal experience in confirmation.**

   o How have you grown?

   o Are you still passionate about teaching the confirmation experience?

   o What will you do differently/better next time?

While the previous timeline does not include all the necessary tasks to prepare for the confirmation experience, it is intended to serve as a general starting point. Your church and its context will influence/change this to-do list. Remember that as much as we plan, we should always save space for the Holy Spirit to work. Also, remember that when your heart is in the right place, "errors" in planning can turn into beautiful God moments. Stay open and God will do the rest.

Things to Remember:

Appendix 2

Reflection Questions

• What are your expectations for the confirmation experience?

•What type of environment do you hope to create?

• What are your goals and expectations for all who will be involved in the confirmation experience?

Parents:

Volunteers:

Mentors:

Clergy:

Staff:

Youth group:

Church:

Yourself:

Students:

Appendix 3

Summary of the Theory of Multiple Intelligences

Based upon his findings from cognitive science and neuroscience research, Howard Gardner determined that there are different cognitive strengths and styles. These cognitive abilities—intelligences—are based upon human biology and psychology, and they represent the various capacities by which individuals process their experiences. Following are descriptions for each of the intelligences.

Logical/Mathematical—ability to order and reorder, identify relationships among abstract ideas. Individuals enjoy puzzles, mathematics, reading, and writing.

Intrapersonal—ability to access one's own feelings, range of emotions in order to label them and draw upon them as a means of guiding one's own behavior. Individuals enjoy personal reflection time, individual vs. team projects, and independence.

Musical—auditory awareness for hearing music. Individuals pay particular attention to rhythm, pitch, and cadences. Individuals enjoy listening to music and performing.

Spatial—ability to reframe visual experiences into multidimensional forms. Individuals enjoy bringing their thoughts to life. They enjoy sketching, building, and sculpting. They also make great chess players.

Linguistic—sensitivity to the order of words—sounds, rhythms, meters of words and languages. Individuals enjoy writing, reading, and listening.

Interpersonal—ability to notice distinctions among others in mood, temperaments, motivations, and intentions. Individuals enjoy interaction with others, group cohesion, and leadership.

Bodily/Kinesthetic—ability to master the use of the body as well as an ability to manipulate objects with finesse. These individuals learn by interacting—dancing, expressing through movement, game playing, and interacting with others.

Naturalist—capacity to recognize distinctions of plants, animals, clouds, and other things in the natural ecological world. Individuals enjoy experiencing nature to identify and study nuances.

—Howard Gardner, *Multiple Intelligences: New Horizons*, completely revised and updated. ed. (New York: Basic Books, 2006); page 5; also Howard Gardner, *Frames of Mind: The Theory of Multiple Intelligences* (New York: Basic Books, 2011).

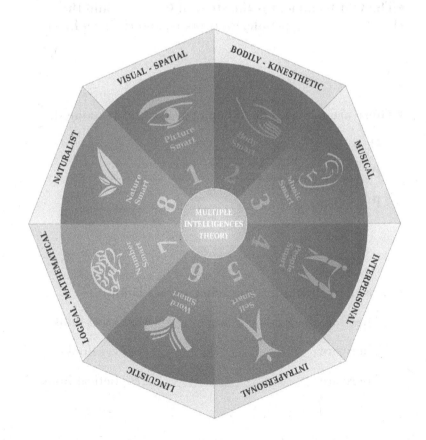

Appendix 4

Understanding the Bible

This is an example of a confirmation handout. The idea is for students to listen and fill in the blanks with key words as a teacher/leader lectures. This was an extra step but, for the special needs student, it was most helpful. It allowed him or her to engage as much as the other students.

• The Old Testament is the story of G_____ and the H_____ people, their poets, and the prophets.

• There are three kinds of books in the Old Testament:

H _____

P _____

P _____

• How many books are in each category below?

There are _____ Historical Books.

There are _____ Poetical Books.

There are _____ Prophetical Books.

• The New Testament is the story of J_____
and the C_____ he founded and its growth under
the leadership of his A _____ after his death.

• What are the three kinds of books in the New Testament?

H _____ books

P _____ Epistles

G _____ Epistles

• How many books of each type are there?

There are _____ Historical books.

There are _____ Pauline Epistles.

There are _____ General Epistles.

Appendix 5: Confirm Unit Summaries

Unit 1: Our Journey

The confirmation journey is about equipping teens with the information, tools, and experiences they need to make an informed decision about committing to follow Christ. The first step (these first four sessions) in that journey is helping your teens to understand the facets of Christian community. Not only will they learn the ins and outs of the United Methodist community, but they will be given the opportunity to build meaningful and powerful relationships with one another, members of their family, and members of their church family. To that end, the first session of this journey is establishing the foundation for meaningful relationships between the teens and their guides for the journey, namely their teachers and mentors. The subsequent two sessions will explore the importance of belonging and participation in the Christian community and challenge the teens to start practicing what it means to live in Christian community. The final session will connect teens with a biblical understanding of belonging. Each step of the way, teens will be challenged to think more deeply about their faith both personally and communally.

Unit 2: Our History and Heritage

In order to truly understand our lives and beliefs we must understand the lives and beliefs of the people who came before us. Our identity and faith is rooted in and shaped by the experiences of our spiritual ancestors traced back over the centuries.

These six lessons are designed to help you consider where your faith comes from in the hope that it will give you a better understanding of where it may be going. You'll be introduced to a long and diverse tradition that you're already part of and encouraged to imagine how you might carry that tradition into the future.

Unit 3: Our Life Together

In this unit your group will jump with both feet into much of what makes the practice of United Methodism unique among other Protestant denominations. We'll explore everything from how our church is organized to how we worship together! Youth will learn about the instrumental role our hymnal plays in preparing for worship, as well as what we believe about our practices of Holy Communion and baptism. The unit then provides an introduction to the United Methodist Social Principles, our guide to being a United Methodist in our world. We close with a reminder that our understanding of social issues is meaningless unless we also take action on what we believe together. Your group will emerge from "Our Life Together" with not only a better understanding of our global church but also with a better understanding of what it means to be confirmed.

Confirm Director Guide

Unit 4: Our Beliefs

Believing in something is taking a step toward the unknown and having the humility to realize that mystery will always be present. It is our human condition to want to know everything; but when we know something, there is no room left for belief. God wants us to believe. The beauty of our relationship with our Creator is that we don't know everything, yet we can trust God—we can trust God to be a part of our lives in ways that we do not understand. And when we truly trust in God, we can then respond in ways that transform the world towards the possibilities of God's kingdom.

What we believe is important—both communally and individually. The United Methodist Church has doctrine that states her institutional beliefs, but she also acknowledges that we are individuals with unique perspectives. Belief is not about being "right" but rather about providing a structure to create a communal identity and a skeletal framework for individual belief. As we take a journey with God, we discover how our church can form our beliefs but also how we individually process our understanding of God.

Creating a Meaningful Confirmation Experience

Unit 5: Our Theology

What we believe as Christians, or our theology, are the
foundational truths that empower us to understand the
Christian faith with both our hearts and minds. This holistic
understanding of our theology empowers us to share the
principals of our faith in meaningful, purposeful ways. Over
the next seven lessons, you will confirm what you may already
know about Jesus, the Holy Spirit, and salvation, as well
as uncover new ways of understanding Christian thoughts
around sin and grace and the rich legacy that a life with
Christ leaves for others to follow into eternity.

Confirm Director Guide

Unit 6: Our Faith and Calling

Our faith and the living out of our faith, also known as our calling, are intricately linked. James 2:17 says, "In the same way, faith is dead when it doesn't result in faithful activity." When we live our faith, our calling is clarified and our relationship with God is strengthened. As our encounters with God clarify who we are, our faith becomes even deeper. We cannot fully understand either faith or calling without the other. This unit will challenge teens to put together all they have been learning over the past sessions and articulate what they believe in their own words. They will be pushed to take their faith and discipleship seriously through realistic examination of the United Methodist baptismal vows and the living out of those vows within the life of their congregation. Ultimately, each teen will have to decide for him or herself if being confirmed in The United Methodist Church is a path he or she is willing and able to take along the faith journey.

Appendix 6

Confirm Scope and Sequence

Your Faith. Your Commitment. God's Call.

UNIT 1 — OUR JOURNEY

Lesson 1: Traveling Together
Lesson 2: Living Together
Lesson 3: Loving Together
Lesson 4: Belonging Together

UNIT 2 — OUR HISTORY AND HERITAGE

Lesson 5: The Faith of Jesus
Lesson 6: The Early Church
Lesson 7: The Reformation
Lesson 8: Wesley and the Methodists
Lesson 9: The Growth of Methodism
Lesson 10: The Local Church

UNIT 3 — OUR LIFE TOGETHER

Lesson 11: The Connection
Lesson 12: Simple Worship
Lesson 13: Music and Lyrics
Lesson 14: Remembrance
Lesson 15: Accepting Grace
Lesson 16: A Loving Church
Lesson 17: So Now What?

RULE 1: DO NO HARM

It is therefore expected of all who continue therein that they should continue to evidence their desire of salvation by **doing no harm**, by avoiding evil of every kind, especially that which is most generally practiced, such as:

- The taking of the name of God in vain.
- The profaning the day of the Lord, either by doing ordinary work therein or by buying or selling.
- Drunkenness: buying or selling spirituous liquors, or drinking them, unless in cases of extreme necessity.
- Slaveholding: buying or selling slaves.
- Fighting, quarreling, brawling, brother going to law with brother; returning evil for evil, or railing for railing; the using many words in buying or selling.
- The buying or selling of goods that have not paid the duty.
- The giving or taking things on usury—i.e., unlawful interest.
- Uncharitable or unprofitable conversation; particularly speaking evil of magistrates or of ministers.
- Doing to others as we would not they should do unto us.
- Doing what we know is not for the glory of God, as:
    - The putting on of gold and costly apparel.
    - The taking such diversions as cannot be used in the name of the Lord Jesus.
    - The singing those songs, or reading those books, which do not tend to the knowledge or love of God.
    - Softness and needless self-indulgence.
    - Laying up treasure upon earth.
    - Borrowing without a probability of paying; or taking up goods without a probability of paying for them.

"Spirituous liquors" is another way of saying "alcoholic beverages."

Railing is an eighteenth-century word for verbal abuse.

Wesley is saying that Christians shouldn't take each other to court. See Matthew 5:23-26.

The more words someone uses in buying and selling, the more likely they are to cheat a person out of money or merchandise.

A duty is a tax placed on certain goods. "Goods that have not paid the duty" are items being sold on the black market.

See Exodus 22:25.

Magistrates and ministers are local and national political leaders.

You may recognize this is a version of the Golden Rule, from Matthew 7:12.

"Laying up treasure upon earth" refers to Jesus's teaching in Matthew 6:19-21 and Luke 12:13-21.

RULE 2: DO GOOD

It is therefore expected of all who continue therein that they should continue to evidence their desire of salvation by **doing good**, by being in every kind merciful after their power; as they have opportunity, doing good of every possible sort, and, as far as possible, to all [people]:

- To their bodies, of the ability which God giveth, by giving food to the hungry, by clothing the naked, by visiting or helping them that are sick or in prison.

- To their souls, by instructing, reproving, or exhorting all we have any intercourse with; trampling under foot that enthusiastic doctrine that "we are not to do good unless our hearts be free to it."

- By doing good, especially to them that are of the household of faith or groaning soon to be; employing them preferably to others; buying one of another, helping each other in business, and so much the more because the world will love its own and them only.

- By all possible diligence and frugality, that the gospel be not blamed.

- By running with patience the race which is set before them, denying themselves, and taking up their cross daily; submitting to bear the reproach of Christ, to be as the filth and offscouring of the world; and looking that men should say all manner of evil of them *falsely*, for the Lord's sake.

The instruction to feed the hungry, clothe the naked, and visit the sick and imprisoned is similar to Jesus's teaching about the judgment of the nations in Matthew 25:34-40.

Wesley rejected the idea that "we are not to do good unless our hearts be free to it" because he believed that all people could choose to do good in all situations. In other words, he believed that God has given people free will.

For more on our responsibilities to those in the "household of faith" (other Christians), see 1 Timothy 5:1–6:2.

Wesley tells Methodists to be diligent and frugal because laziness and greed would reflect poorly on God and the church.

Offscouring means "that which is disposed of."

"Running with patience the race which is set before them" comes from Hebrews 12:1.

In other words, faithful Christians shouldn't be surprised if they're the subject of nasty lies.

RULE 3: STAY IN LOVE WITH GOD

It is therefore expected of all who continue therein that they should continue to evidence their desire of salvation by **attending upon all the ordinances of God**; such are:

- The public worship of God.
- The ministry of the Word, either read or expounded.
- The Supper of the Lord.
- Family and private prayer.
- Searching the Scriptures.
- Fasting or abstinence.

This, in other words, means "go to church."

The word *expounded* includes listening to sermons

This is also known as Holy Communion or the Eucharist.

Fasting and abstinence aren't limited to refraining from food and sexual activity. A person could also fast from television or their phone; someone could abstain from insulting others or complaining.

USEFUL TERMS AND CONCEPTS FOR UNITED METHODISTS (CHURCHY WORDS)

Acolyte: a person who assists in the worship service. Normally the acolyte serves by lighting and extinguishing the candles on the Communion or altar table and distributing and collecting the offering plates.

Advent: a season of preparation for Christ's promised coming; begins on the fourth Sunday before Christmas

Aldersgate: from Aldersgate Street in London. On this street was a meeting place in which John Wesley had his heart-warming conversion experience on May 24, 1738. Charles Wesley also had a conversion experience in the same place, only a few days before.

Annual Conference: a regional, organizational unit of The United Methodist Church and the yearly business meeting of that unit, presided over by a bishop. The business session is composed of equal numbers of clergy and laity. At least one layperson from each pastoral charge is a member. There are 63 annual conferences in the United States and 59 outside the United States in Africa, Europe, and the Philippines. The conference is a time to review ministry, adopt policy and resolutions, and strengthen spiritual life.

Apostles' Creed: an ancient statement of belief still used by many Christian denominations and included in the confirmation vows of The United Methodist Church. The Apostles' Creed is arranged in three sections, one for each person of the Trinity.

Apportionment: the share each annual conference or local church pays to support international, national, and regional mission

Arminian/Arminianism: belief favored in Methodist teaching that God intends the salvation of all human beings and that Christ died for all human beings

Ash Wednesday: the first day of Lent. Ash Wednesday gets its name from the tradition of placing ashes on people's foreheads as a sign of repentance. (Repentance is an important theme during the Lenten season.)

Assurance: historic Methodist teaching maintaining that when a person is justified, they experience divine assurance of the forgiveness of sins. In other words, they know they have been forgiven.

Atonement: the act of sinners being restored and reconciled to God through Jesus's death on the cross. The term is translated as "reconciliation" in the CEB.

Baptism: an initiation into Christ's body, the church, that involves being ritually cleansed by water

Baptismal Font: the basin of water used in baptism by sprinkling and pouring

Body of Christ: a metaphor that the apostle Paul uses to describe the church in 1 Corinthians 12:12-27. Paul says that each member of the church is a different part of Christ's body. Because we are Christ's body, we must act as Christ's eyes, ears, hands, feet, and heart in the world.

Book of Discipline, The: a fundamental book outlining the law, doctrine, administration, organizational work, and procedures of The United Methodist Church. Each General Conference amends The Book of Discipline, and the actions of the General Conference are reflected in the quadrennial revision. Often referred to as The Discipline.

Book of Resolutions, The: the volume containing the text of all resolutions or pronouncements on issues approved by the General Conference and currently valid. The text of any resolution is considered the official position of the denomination on that subject.

Cabinet: the resident bishop and district superintendents within an annual conference. The cabinet provides oversight and direction for the work of the annual conference, districts, and local churches.

Central Conference: one of eight geographic areas outside the territorial United States, each composed of annual conferences as determined by the General Conference. Central conferences have responsibilities similar to those of jurisdictional conferences. The eight central conferences are in Europe, Africa, and Asia.

Charge Conference: the charge conference is the basic governing body of each United Methodist local church and is composed of all members of the church council. All members of the charge conference must be members of the local church. The charge conference directs the work of the church and gives general oversight to the church council, reviews and evaluates the mission and ministry of the church, sets salaries for the pastor and staff, elects the members of the church council, and recommends candidates for ordained ministry.

Christ: literally means "anointed one"; Jesus of Nazareth, who was fully human and fully God; the person of the Trinity who redeems us and calls us brothers, sisters, and friends

Christian Perfection: see "Sanctification"

Christmas: celebration of Jesus's birth. The Christmas season lasts from Christmas Eve until January 5, the day before Epiphany.

Christmas Conference: the name given to the conference at which the Methodist Episcopal Church in America was formally organized. The conference began on December 24, 1784, and lasted until January 2 or 3, 1785, at the Lovely Lane Chapel in Baltimore, Maryland.

Church: a community of Christian believers who gather in Jesus's name to worship, learn about God, discern God's will, and serve God's people

Circuit Rider: a historic term in American Methodism. From the earliest years of the denomination, pastors were appointed to serve numerous local churches and other preaching places located within a large geographic area. These ministers traveled regularly throughout their assigned areas and came to be known as circuit riders.

Clergy: individuals who serve as commissioned ministers, deacons, elders, and local pastors under appointment of a bishop (full- and part-time), who hold membership in an annual conference, and who are commissioned, ordained, or licensed

Communion Elements: the bread and wine (or juice) used in Holy Communion

Compassion: caring for the physical, spiritual, and emotional needs of others

Confess: to honestly admit one's mistakes; to profess one's faith

Connection: the principle, basic to The United Methodist Church, that all leaders and congregations are connected in a network of loyalties and commitments

Creation: God's handiwork; the entire universe, from the smallest particle to the largest galaxy

Creed: a formal statement of belief

Deacon: an ordained clergyperson who is called to serve all people, particularly people who are poor, sick, and oppressed, and to equip and lead the laity in ministries of compassion, justice, and service in the world

Delegate: a pastor or layperson elected by an annual conference as its representative to General Conference, jurisdictional conference, or central conference

Discernment: a process of prayer, study, and reflection for the purpose of making decisions and knowing God's will

Discipline: activities and exercises that help a person develop a skill or behavior; rules and guidelines that govern how a person lives; an unwavering commitment to certain activities, exercises, rules, and/or guidelines (see "Book of Discipline, The")

District Superintendent: an ordained minister appointed by a bishop to oversee the pastors and local churches in a district

Easter: celebrates Christ's resurrection. The Easter season is from Easter Sunday until Pentecost, the fiftieth day after Easter.

Elder: a person ordained to a lifetime ministry of service, word, sacrament, and order. He or she is authorized to preach and teach God's word, administer the sacraments of baptism and Holy Communion, and order the life of the church for mission and ministry.

Epiphany: January 6, the day on which Christians celebrate the visit of the magi (or wise men)

Eucharist: literally means "thanksgiving"; a name for the sacrament of Holy Communion

Evil: that which causes harm and goes against God's will

Faith: belief combined with heartfelt trust

Falling from Grace: informal term for the Methodist doctrine that an individual can lose faith in Christ and forfeit their justification

Freedom, Free Will: our God-given ability to choose to accept God's grace or resist it

General Agency: any council, board, commission, committee, or other unit established to carry out denominational work. General agencies are accountable to the General Conference.

General Conference: The highest legislative body in The United Methodist Church. The voting membership consists of an equal number of clergy and lay delegates elected by the annual conferences. General Conference convenes every quadrennium (four years) to determine the denomination's future direction. It's the only body that can speak officially for the denomination.

Gifts: the abilities and resources God blesses us with

Holiness: being empowered by the Holy Spirit to be fully devoted to God and to live according to God's will

Creating a Meaningful Confirmation Experience

Holy Spirit: the person of the Trinity who guides us, sustains us, and comforts us; often described using the metaphors of wind and breath

Hymnal, The United Methodist: the current hymnal was approved by the 1988 General Conference and was published in 1989. The 2016 General Conference approved the plan for a new hymnal that is to be presented at the 2020 General Conference and published in 2021. Hymnals have been important in the life of the Wesleyan movement from the very beginning. John Wesley published his first hymnal in 1737 in South Carolina.

Image of God (Imago Dei): the concept that humans reflect God's likeness, as demonstrated by our abilities to love and create (see Genesis 1:27)

Infant Baptism: the practice of baptizing infants and small children because baptism is a work of God's grace, and God's grace is present in people's lives even before they're aware of it. The United Methodist Church affirms and practices infant baptism, as do the Roman Catholic, Eastern Orthodox, Anglican, Lutheran, and Presbyterian Churches.

Intercessory Prayer: prayer on behalf of another person

Intinction: the act of dipping Communion bread into the cup

Itineracy, Itinerancy: the system in The United Methodist Church by which pastors are appointed to their charges by bishops. The pastors are under obligation to serve where appointed. Itinerant means traveling or moving from place to place.

Judicial Council: nine people elected by General Conference who rule on questions of constitutionality in church law and practice

Jurisdiction: five geographic areas in the United States, each composed of several annual conferences as determined by the General Conference: North Central, Northeastern, South Central, Southeastern, and Western

Jurisdictional Conference: the quadrennial meeting of clergy and lay delegates from the annual conferences within the boundaries of each of the five US jurisdictions. Their business includes the election and assignment of bishops.

Justice: seeking peace and wholeness for all people and all of God's creation, making God's kingdom present on earth

Justification, Justifying Grace: the grace that brings us into right relationship with God. Our responsibility is to respond to God's grace in faith and make a decision to follow Christ. Prevenient grace leads us to justifying grace. Methodist doctrine holds that our justification is by grace through faith.

Kingdom of God: the vision of a world totally aligned to God's will that is governed by God's love and justice. Jesus often taught about God's kingdom and described it in parables. Revelation 21:1–22:5 gives us a vision of this kingdom in its description of a new heaven and new earth.

Laity: from the Greek word laos, meaning "people," and used to describe members of a congregation or parish

Lectionary: a guide for worship that prescribes certain scripture readings for each Sunday throughout the Christian year. Many United Methodist congregations use the Revised Common Lectionary, which usually suggests an Old Testament reading, a Psalm, a Gospel reading, and a reading from one of the New Testament letters for each week.

Lent: recalls Jesus's forty-day temptation in the wilderness and journey toward Jerusalem and the cross. The forty days (not including Sundays) of Lent begin with Ash Wednesday and continue through Holy Week.

Liturgy: a pattern of public worship performed by the people of a congregation

Means of Grace: the normal means, or channels, by which God conveys grace to human beings, including the Lord's Supper, Bible study, prayer, and fasting

Methodist, Methodism: two words, along with Wesleyan, used to describe the movement resulting from the work of John Wesley and his brother Charles. The movement had its very earliest expression in the Holy Club at Oxford. There John and Charles Wesley and others joined together in a highly structured and disciplined pattern of worship, prayer, and study. Those outside the group derisively called the groups "Methodists" because of their methodical approach to their religion. The name was later applied to the followers of the Wesleys as they actively preached throughout England. Methodist and Methodism are used to refer to a large family of churches and denominations throughout the world.

Missionary: A lay- or clergyperson selected and commissioned to serve in the work of The United Methodist Church or related denominations in other lands or in designated projects in the United States. Missionaries are selected, assigned, and directed in their work by the General Board of Global Ministries.

Nicene Creed: an ancient statement of Christian belief adopted by the fourth-century Council of Nicaea. The council wrote the creed for the purpose of it being a standard of correct Christian belief. The Nicene Creed is arranged in three sections, one for each person of the Trinity. The creed emphasizes that Jesus Christ is both fully human and fully divine and explains how the persons of the Trinity relate to each other.

Open Communion: the long-standing custom of Methodist churches sharing the Lord's Supper with members of other churches

Ordinary Time: a time to reflect on doing the work of God's kingdom and growing spiritually. Ordinary Time falls between Pentecost and the beginning of Advent.

Ordination: the act of conferring ministerial orders, presided over by a bishop; the authorization of the church for the practice of service, word, sacrament, and order (in the case of an elder) and for the practice of word and service (in the case of a deacon)

Original Sin: Methodist doctrine affirms original sin as the "corruption of nature" within every human being that leads to actual sin. Methodist doctrine does not formally endorse the belief that original sin itself warrants eternal damnation.

Paraments: decorations in a sanctuary or worship space in colors that correspond to the seasons of the Christian year

Pentecost: commemorates the outpouring of the Holy Spirit and the establishment of the church. Pentecost is the fiftieth day after Easter.

Prayer: a spiritual practice in which we communicate and spend time with God. Prayer can be individual or communal, and prayer involves both taking things to God and listening in silence.

Prayers of Confession: prayers in which we take our sins before God and give thanks for the forgiveness we have through Christ

Prayers of Petition: prayers in which we take our concerns to God

Lent: recalls Jesus's forty-day temptation in the wilderness and journey toward Jerusalem and the cross. The forty days (not including Sundays) of Lent begin with Ash Wednesday and continue through Holy Week.

Liturgy: a pattern of public worship performed by the people of a congregation

Means of Grace: the normal means, or channels, by which God conveys grace to human beings, including the Lord's Supper, Bible study, prayer, and fasting

Methodist, Methodism: two words, along with Wesleyan, used to describe the movement resulting from the work of John Wesley and his brother Charles. The movement had its very earliest expression in the Holy Club at Oxford. There John and Charles Wesley and others joined together in a highly structured and disciplined pattern of worship, prayer, and study. Those outside the group derisively called the groups "Methodists" because of their methodical approach to their religion. The name was later applied to the followers of the Wesleys as they actively preached throughout England. Methodist and Methodism are used to refer to a large family of churches and denominations throughout the world.

Missionary: A lay- or clergyperson selected and commissioned to serve in the work of The United Methodist Church or related denominations in other lands or in designated projects in the United States. Missionaries are selected, assigned, and directed in their work by the General Board of Global Ministries.

Nicene Creed: an ancient statement of Christian belief adopted by the fourth-century Council of Nicaea. The council wrote the creed for the purpose of it being a standard of correct Christian belief. The Nicene Creed is arranged in three sections, one for each person of the Trinity. The creed emphasizes that Jesus Christ is both fully human and fully divine and explains how the persons of the Trinity relate to each other.

Open Communion: the long-standing custom of Methodist churches sharing the Lord's Supper with members of other churches

Ordinary Time: a time to reflect on doing the work of God's kingdom and growing spiritually. Ordinary Time falls between Pentecost and the beginning of Advent.

Ordination: the act of conferring ministerial orders, presided over by a bishop; the authorization of the church for the practice of service, word, sacrament, and order (in the case of an elder) and for the practice of word and service (in the case of a deacon)

Original Sin: Methodist doctrine affirms original sin as the "corruption of nature" within every human being that leads to actual sin. Methodist doctrine does not formally endorse the belief that original sin itself warrants eternal damnation.

Paraments: decorations in a sanctuary or worship space in colors that correspond to the seasons of the Christian year

Pentecost: commemorates the outpouring of the Holy Spirit and the establishment of the church. Pentecost is the fiftieth day after Easter.

Prayer: a spiritual practice in which we communicate and spend time with God. Prayer can be individual or communal, and prayer involves both taking things to God and listening in silence.

Prayers of Confession: prayers in which we take our sins before God and give thanks for the forgiveness we have through Christ

Prayers of Petition: prayers in which we take our concerns to God

Stewardship: faithfully managing and caring for the things God has entrusted to us

United Methodist Church, The: this denomination was formed in 1968 by the union of The Evangelical United Brethren Church and The Methodist Church. It serves members in more than seventy annual conferences in five jurisdictional conferences in the United States and nearly forty annual and provisional annual conferences in eight central conferences in Africa, Europe, and Asia.

Universal Availability of Grace: the idea that God intends for all human beings to be saved and makes grace (prevenient grace) available to all

Universal Need for Grace: human beings cannot save themselves and thus all need divine grace or assistance

Way of Salvation: the process of salvation from the beginnings of God's work under prevenient grace through justification and sanctification, as expressed in historic Methodist doctrinal statements and in the structure of Methodist hymnals

Wesleyan Quadrilateral: using the Bible, tradition, reason, and experience as a method for theological reflection. Although John Wesley himself didn't lay out of the quadrilateral as such, he did use scripture, reason, and experience, and he referenced particular moments from the Christian past. The Wesleyan quadrilateral was first expressed in the UM statement of Our Theological Task in The Book of Discipline.

Witness: the way in which Christians, through our words and example, show the world God's redeeming love through Christ

Worship: the means by which a community of faith praises and gives thanks to God, confesses their sins, participates in the sacraments of baptism and Holy Communion, and receives guidance and nourishment from the Holy Spirit

PREAMBLE TO THE SOCIAL PRINCIPLES OF THE UNITED METHODIST CHURCH

[The Social Principles are ¶¶160–166 of the *Book of Discipline*. They are "not to be considered church law but are a prayerful and thoughtful effort on the part of the General Conference to speak to the human issues in the contemporary world from a sound biblical and theological foundation as historically demonstrated in United Methodist traditions."]

We, the people called United Methodists, affirm our faith in God our Creator and Father, in Jesus Christ our Savior, and in the Holy Spirit, our Guide and Guard.

We acknowledge our complete dependence upon God in birth, in life, in death, and in life eternal. Secure in God's love, we affirm the goodness of life and confess our many sins against God's will for us as we find it in Jesus Christ. We have not always been faithful stewards of all that has been committed to us by God the Creator. We have been reluctant followers of Jesus Christ in his mission to bring all persons into a community of love. Though called by the Holy Spirit to become new creatures in Christ, we have resisted the further call to become the people of God in our dealings with each other and the earth on which we live.

We affirm our unity in Jesus Christ while acknowledging differences in applying our faith in different cultural contexts as we live out the gospel.

Grateful for God's forgiving love, in which we live and by which we are judged, and affirming our belief in the inestimable worth of each individual, we renew our commitment to become faithful witnesses to the gospel, not alone to the ends of the earth, but also to the depths of our common life and work.

OUR SOCIAL CREED

[This statement is the final paragraph of the Social Principles in The Book of Discipline. At its end is a note reading: "It is recommended that this statement of Social Principles be continually available to United Methodist Christians and that it be emphasized regularly in every congregation. It is further recommended that , 'Our Social Creed', be frequently used in Sunday worship."]

We believe in God, Creator of the world; and in Jesus Christ, the Redeemer of creation. We believe in the Holy Spirit, through whom we acknowledge God's gifts, and we repent of our sin in misusing these gifts to idolatrous ends.

We affirm the natural world as God's handiwork and dedicate ourselves to its preservation, enhancement, and faithful use by humankind.

We joyfully receive for ourselves and others the blessings of community, sexuality, marriage, and the family.

We commit ourselves to the rights of men, women, children, youth, young adults, the aging, and people with disabilities; to improvement of the quality of life; and to the rights and dignity of all persons.

We believe in the right and duty of persons to work for the glory of God and the good of themselves and others and in the protection of their welfare in so doing; in the rights to property as a trust from God, collective bargaining, and responsible consumption; and in the elimination of economic and social distress.

We dedicate ourselves to peace throughout the world, to the rule of justice and law among nations, and to individual freedom for all people of the world.

We believe in the present and final triumph of God's Word in human affairs and gladly accept our commission to manifest the life of the gospel in the world. Amen.

CONFIRMATION VOWS

Do you renounce the spiritual forces of wickedness,
reject the evil powers of this world,
and repent of your sin?

I do.

Do you accept the freedom and power God gives you to resist evil, injustice, and oppression in whatever forms they present themselves?

I do.

Do you confess Jesus Christ as your Savior,
put your whole trust in his grace,
and promise to serve him as your Lord,
in union with the Church which Christ has opened
to people of all ages, nations, and races?

I do.

Bibliography

Anders, Max E. *30 Days to Understanding the Bible in 15 Minutes a Day!* new expanded ed. Nashville, TN.: T. Nelson, 1998.

Browning, Robert L., and Roy A. Reed. *Models of Confirmation and Baptismal Affirmation: Liturgical and Educational Issues and Designs*. Birmingham, AL.: Religious Education Press, 1995.

Brueggemann, Walter. *The Creative Word: Canon as a Model for Biblical Education*. Philadelphia, PA.: Fortress Press, 1982.

Clark, Chap. *Hurt 2.0: Inside the World of Today's Teenagers. Youth, Family, and Culture Series*. Grand Rapids, MI.: Baker Academic, 2011.

Dix, Dom Gregory. *The Theology of Confirmation in Relation to Baptism*. Westminster: Dacre Press, 1946. Public lecture at the University of Oxford; delivered on January 22, 1946.

Epstein, Robert. *The Case Against Adolescence: Rediscovering the Adult in Every Teen*. Sanger, CA.: Quill Driver Books/Word Dancer Press, 2007.

Felton, Gayle Carlton. *By Water and the Spirit: Making Connections for Identity and Ministry*. study ed. Nashville, TN.: Discipleship Resources, 1997.

Fisher, John Douglas Close. *Christian Initiation: Confirmation Then and Now. Classics Series*. Chicago, IL.: Hillenbrand Books, 2005.

Foster, Charles R. *From Generation to Generation: The Adaptive Challenge of Mainline Protestant Education in Forming Faith*. Eugene, OR.: Cascade Books, 2012.

Hewer, C T R. *Understanding Islam: An Introduction*. Minneapolis, MN.: Fortress Press, 2006.

Kavanagh, Aidan. *Confirmation: Origins and Reform*. New York, NY.: Pueblo Pub. Co., 1988.

Leneman, Cantor Helen. *Bar/Bat Mitzvah Basics, 2nd Ed.: a Practical Family Guide to Coming of Age Together.* Woodstock, VT.: Jewish Lights Publishing, 2011.

Mead, Margaret. *Coming of Age in Samoa: A Psychological Study of Primitive Youth for Western Civilization*. New York, NY.: Perennial Classics, 2001.

Myers, William, and Gary Halstead, eds. *Becoming and Belonging: A Practical Design for Confirmation*. Cleveland, OH.: United Church Press, 1993.

Osmer, Richard Robert. *Confirmation: Presbyterian Practices in Ecumenical Perspective*. Louisville, KY.: Geneva Press, 1996.

Palmer, Parker J. *A Hidden Wholeness: The Journey Toward an Undivided Life*. San Francisco, CA.: Jossey-Bass, 2004.

Steegstra, Marijke. *Modernity and Belonging. Vol. 3, Resilient Rituals: Krobo Initiation and the Politics of Culture in Ghana*. Münster: Lit, 2004.

Vygotsky, L S. *Mind in Society: The Development of Higher Psychological Processes*. Edited Michael Cole. Cambridge: Harvard University Press, 1978.

CPSIA information can be obtained
at www.ICGtesting.com
Printed in the USA
LVHW090628110922
728033LV00004B/11

9 781501 826924